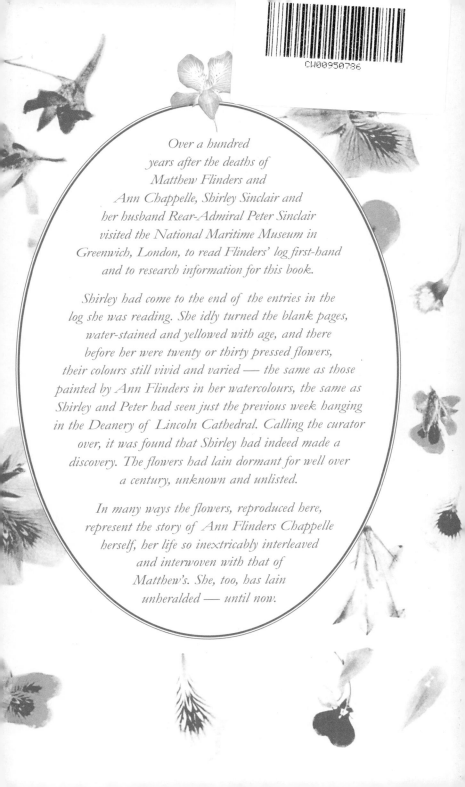

Over a hundred
years after the deaths of
Matthew Flinders and
Ann Chappelle, Shirley Sinclair and
her husband Rear-Admiral Peter Sinclair
visited the National Maritime Museum in
Greenwich, London, to read Flinders' log first-hand
and to research information for this book.

Shirley had come to the end of the entries in the
log she was reading. She idly turned the blank pages,
water-stained and yellowed with age, and there
before her were twenty or thirty pressed flowers,
their colours still vivid and varied — the same as those
painted by Ann Flinders in her watercolours, the same as
Shirley and Peter had seen just the previous week hanging
in the Deanery of Lincoln Cathedral. Calling the curator
over, it was found that Shirley had indeed made a
discovery. The flowers had lain dormant for well over
a century, unknown and unlisted.

In many ways the flowers, reproduced here,
represent the story of Ann Flinders Chappelle
herself, her life so inextricably interleaved
and interwoven with that of
Matthew's. She, too, has lain
unheralded — until now.

Letters to Ann

The love story of
Matthew Flinders
and Ann Chappelle

CATHARINE RETTER & SHIRLEY SINCLAIR

Angus&Robertson
An imprint of HarperCollins*Publishers*

~ For the two Peters: Peter Retter and Peter Sinclair ~

The artwork on pages 39 and 129 is reproduced by
the kind permission of Flinders University of South Australia.

Angus&Robertson

An imprint of HarperCollins*Publishers*, Australia
First published in Australia in 1999
by HarperCollins*Publishers* Pty Limited
ACN 009 013 517
A member of the HarperCollins*Publishers* (Australia) Pty Limited Group
http://www.harpercollins.com.au

Text copyright © Catharine Retter 1999

HarperCollins*Publishers*
25 Ryde Road, Pymble, Sydney, NSW 2073, Australia
31 View Road, Glenfield, Auckland 10, New Zealand
77–85 Fulham Palace Road, London W6 8JB, United Kingdom
Hazelton Lanes, 55 Avenue Road, Suite 2900, Toronto, Ontario M5R 3L2
and 1995 Markham Road, Scarborough, Ontario M1B 5M8, Canada
10 East 53rd Street, New York NY 10032, USA

National Library of Australia Cataloguing-in-Publication data:

Retter, Catharine
Letters to Ann: the love story of Matthew Flinders and Ann Chappelle.
Bibliography.
ISBN 0 207 196966
1. Flinders, Matthew, 1774-1814. 2. Flinders, Matthew, 1774–1814 –
Marriage. 3. Chapelle, Ann. 4. Explorers – Family relationships.
I. Sinclair, Shirley, 1934– . II. Title.

Produced in Australia by Griffin Press Pty Ltd on 66gsm Suma Book Cream
5 4 3 2 1   02 01 00 99 98

Acknowledgements

Catharine Retter and Shirley Sinclair are indebted to Lisette Flinders Petrie for access to the manuscript in her keeping, for her generous help across the Internet, her reading of our manuscript and her kind permission to reproduce the silhouettes of Ann and Matthew Flinders as well as the watercolouring of Ann, Isabella Tyler and daughter Anne.

The authors would also like to express their heartfelt thanks and appreciation to the many other people who helped in making this book a reality, in particular:

Jacqueline Chalker, Government House, Sydney, Australia; Royal Australian Historical Society; Rex Davis, Sub Dean, Lincoln Cathedral; Clive Powell, Manuscript Subject Specialist, National Maritime Museum, Greenwich; Liz Hill, Australia House, The Strand, London; Nan and the late Geoffrey C Ingleton, Parramatta, Australia.

Authors' notes

In researching this story during a visit to England in April 1996 there were several special occasions which helped bring me close to Ann and Matthew. The discovery of the pressed flowers in the log was one. Another was our visit to the old Norman church of St Nicholas in Partney where they were married. A small but proud English country church, St Nicholas has been the focal point of the village for six centuries. Old gravestones rest under oak trees said to be hundreds of years old, and the church itself has probably changed little, if at all, since Ann and Matthew married there. By chance, my husband and I visited St Nicholas on 17th April 1996, their 195th wedding anniversary. I like to think that Ann and Matthew would have been pleased that an Australian Navy man and his wife were there on that day to remember them.

Shirley Sinclair

*T*his story, told in part through the many and endearing love letters of Matthew Flinders to his sweetheart and wife, is a tribute to their enduring if somewhat storm-tossed love as well as to the woman whose kind nature, strength of character and strength of belief in him did not waver in more than nine long years of absence and thirteen short years of marriage. Not just their love but the true story of their deep friendship brings history to life more than any work of fiction can do.

So little has been directly chronicled of Ann Flinders that much of her story must be told through the eyes and pen of her husband. On the other hand, much has already been written elsewhere of Flinders' exploits in the *Investigator* and in the *Reliance*, his circumnavigation of Tasmania with his friend George Bass, his discovery of Spencer's Gulf and Kangaroo Island, his surveying of the Gulf of Carpentaria and the first circumnavigation of Australia. This book therefore does not attempt to re-chronicle those achievements. However, some of his lesser-known, his personal and even his more disastrous experiences have been told here because of their inescapable impact upon the woman he left behind, to whom he wrote of his anguish, his fears, despair and love.

Catharine Retter

Preface

In 1814 a delicately pale Englishwoman of uncertain health but most certain convictions sat at her desk and wrote a letter of protest to history about her husband Matthew Flinders. '*The disaster of his life,*' she wrote, '*has followed him even into death.*' Her presence on his ship had once caused stern rebuke from his patron Sir Joseph Banks. He had survived shipwreck on two occasions before being imprisoned by the French, causing a separation of nine and a half years from his wife after just three months' marriage. Now, on his death, the Lords of the Admiralty had left his widow pensionless. '*He died if ever Man did, a martyr to his zeal for his country's service,*' Ann Flinders Chappelle wrote sadly of her husband.

His life, his disasters, his martyrdom were also her own. In life Matthew had acknowledged their inseparability, though writing to her from two oceans away: '*thou art a part of me. Thy joys, thy pleasures, or pains are also mine . . . I love thee most tenderly.*'

A woman in nineteenth-century England had few ways to right an injustice. Ann did what little she could. She set down an account of Matthew Flinders' exploits for future generations — for her child and future grandchild. Unbeknown to her, she was also writing for the generations to come of historians and schoolchildren, and for unborn Australians who gladly gave a place in history to the man who charted and named their homeland.

During Matthew's lifetime Sir Joseph Banks, also an important figure in Australian history, saw in Flinders a man of determination and single-minded ambition, a man who would not disappoint his patron. The Lords of the Admiralty, however, saw in him only a brave and somewhat foolhardy adventurer. Flinders' journals and his revealing letters show him to be a man who loved enduringly and passionately, yet Ann once wrote of him, *'no difficulty could stop his career, no danger dismay him: hunger, thirst, labour, rest, sickness, shipwreck, imprisonment, Death itself, were equally to him matters of indifference if they interfered with his darling Discovery.'*

Matthew Flinders was also a man before his time. Just before their marriage he wrote to Ann exhorting her to:

> *learn music, learn the French language, enlarge the subjects of thy pencil, study geography and astronomy and even metaphysics, sooner than leave thy mind unoccupied. Soar, my Annette, aspire to the heights of science. Write a great deal, work with thy needle a great deal, and read every book that comes in thy way, save trifling novels.*

Ann was fortunate to have been born into the latter half of the eighteenth century, for no longer was it sufficient for a wife to be just a decorative accessory to her husband or an efficient housekeeper. Among gentlefolk, a woman was now expected to be able to converse intelligently and become a true companion to the traditionally educated males in the family. The education of young women was therefore looked upon quite favourably — both in formal schooling and less formally in the continuing acquisition of knowledge gained through reading and a curious mind. A young lady's education, deemed necessary to make her a worthy companion (but certainly not to prepare her for the world or for a career), now consisted of a knowledge of geography, history, literature, languages, and arithmetic sufficient for household budgeting. She was, of course, also required to be accomplished in dancing, deportment and needlework. For those who could afford it, it was common practice to employ private teachers, and schools for young ladies flourished. Booksellers' shops were frequented by men and women alike, although the reading of novels was still considered wanton and somewhat dangerous. The literature of Shakespeare, Dr Johnson, Smollett, Fielding and Goldsmith was popular. It was also the age in which Jane Austen lived and wrote.

History records variations on the spelling of words and names used in this book, and we have endeavoured to remain true to the spellings used by Ann and Matthew Flinders themselves in their writings. The French spelling of 'Chappelle' was changed to 'Chappell' not long after Ann and Matthew's generation, probably to anglicise the language after the wars with France. We also note that Matthew Flinders' spellings of the names of people and places are not always correct, but where he is being quoted we have followed his lead. Likewise, punctuation was less formal in Ann and Matthew's day, but we have retained their usage in our quest for authenticity.

CONTENTS

1

Charming sisters, disagreeable brothers

Before her marriage, Ann Chappelle was a woman typical of her time. She was educated sufficiently to converse intelligently, but not enough to place her intellectually above eligible prospects. She had been just four years old when her father, John Chappelle, died. He was forty, a courteous and gentle-natured man, slight, gracious and cultivated. Among the rough North Sea sailors he was known as '*the Gentleman Captain*'. He had married Anne Mallison, a descendant of a Norman baronet turned regicide who had helped sign the death warrant of Charles I.

In 1772, the year of Captain James Cook's second journey of discovery south, on 21st November a baby girl was born to them — Ann Chappelle.

John Chappelle so loved books and poetry that he never put to sea without his much-read copy of *Paradise Lost* or the pensive wanderings of Edward Young's *Night-Thoughts on Life, Death & Immortality*. From these he drew solace on the long evenings in his cabin away from his wife and only child. However, during his adult life John Chappelle suffered from severely debilitating headaches, and in late November 1776, just six years after his marriage, he died in agony in his ship at sea, a towel around his head.

The young child he left behind could not have remembered much of her seafaring father, but she did recall the heartache, the hardship and the loss that were the legacy of his passing. She remembered it sufficiently in later life not to want to link her fate to the long, lonely and uncertain years which faced the sweetheart or wife of a seaman.

Ann inherited her father's slight build, his raven black curly hair, dark eyes and gentle nature. However, fate as well as genetics were to repeat themselves, for not only did she eventually marry a sailor and bear him a daughter, Anne, but like her mother, her marriage was also cut sadly short. Unhappily, too, she inherited the headaches that had plagued her father, and must have lived in fear of ending her life in similar agony.

Her mother was a rather stern but kind woman, stout, dignified and somewhat florid in complexion. She was regarded as '*one of the old type*', and instilled in her daughter the Puritan principles of theology and punctuality, sprinkled liberally with a love of poetry and literature.

The young Ann was fortunate that her mother, the eldest of nine children, was a capable and practical soul used to managing a household and caring for others. Sustained by John's limited savings, the widow and young daughter lived a quiet and sheltered life, participating in village and church activities. Around this time a Reverend William Tyler moved to the district and purchased a house in Partney. Eventually his kind ways and dedication to his flock made him much loved by the villagers and farmers alike. Brought together by church activities, William Tyler and the widowed Anne became friends and then, to the delight of their families, decided to marry.

William Tyler cared for his young stepdaughter as though she were his own, and he was to abruptly learn the responsibilities of his newfound fatherhood when Ann contracted smallpox. A grave and putrid disease, smallpox was common in eighteenth-century England. Blistering sores spread over Ann's pale young body, one sore erupting in her eye having to be lanced. Thus at age twelve, according to family records, Ann lost the sight of the eye, but apart from some possible scarring, otherwise appeared to have recovered well.

Two years later, at fourteen years of age, Ann became a sister when her mother gave birth to Isabella. From the outset the half-sisters were constant companions, and the two remained close and good friends throughout their lives. While Ann cared for her sister at the beginning of her young life, Isabella was by Ann's side tending to her at the close of hers. With Ann helping to raise Isabella, Mrs Tyler was able to assist her spouse in his studies and pastoral duties, and as a result came to be highly esteemed by all who knew her — parishioners and clergy alike.

In the village of Donington, over 30 miles away from the Tylers, Dr Flinders, a stern frugal man, lived with Elizabeth Weekes — his second wife — and five children, of whom Matthew was the eldest son. By most accounts, the stepmother did not have a happy relationship with her children.

Elizabeth, Matthew's closest sister, married a much older man, supposedly to escape the influence of her stepmother. It was not a happy marriage and Elizabeth died at twenty-four from what was then referred to as a '*decline*'; but family lore has it that this would be more aptly described as '*mental suffering*' inflicted by her husband. There was also friction between the other sister, Susanna, and her parents. She was not highly educated but was sensible and clever and she wrote a number of essays, which were published after her death. To her father's dismay, she married a man he considered beneath her when, aged twenty-three, she wed George Pearson, a journeyman draper and Calvinist Methodist. However, it was by all reports a successful marriage and resulted in eight children, two of whom (Susanna Pilgrim and Eliza Jackson) later emigrated to Australia.

John, the eldest of Matthew's brothers and seven years his junior, was referred to by his father as '*my unfortunate John*', and from an early age he led an idle, drunken and dissipated life. According to family records, his appearance was '*not agreeable*' and he was '*dull, perverse, obstinate, weak and untoward*'. At age nineteen he was diagnosed as insane and sent to the York Castle Lunatic Asylum, where he remained until his death.

The remaining brother, Samuel Ward Flinders, followed Matthew to sea and sailed with him in the *Reliance*, and was later a lieutenant in the *Investigator*. He was clever in mathematics and in nautical calculations, and there were those who recognised him as an accomplished navigator and surveyor, indispensable to Matthew in his chartmaking. Others saw him as being lazy and obstinate, allowing the ship's chronometers to run down during crucial survey work along the Australian coast. A worse crime is difficult to imagine, for once wound down, a chronometer could not be accurately reset until the ship called into port or chanced to meet another ship at sea. So crucial is a chronometer to calculations of longitude that it is wound at exactly the same time each day, with the same number of turns, and its winding is entered in a special log.

Samuel married at age forty and raised a family of three daughters and a son. Matthew's grandson was later to write of his great-uncle as *'idle, selfish, quarrelsome — an unkind brother, husband and father'*.

As the eldest son, Matthew was supposed to follow in his father's profession as a physician, in the tradition of three successive generations of Flinders. As a profession it was viewed quite differently then to how it is regarded today. To be a physician or surgeon was to follow an inexact science and it involved a degree of physical work. Service to one's country as an officer in the army or even the navy was considered a far more attractive career.

According to Ann's memoir, at age twelve Matthew was sent to a grammar school in Warbling to acquire *'a competent knowledge of the greek and latin classics'*. He continued at Warbling for three years before being taken home by his father for *'initiation in the mysteries of physic'*. Matthew, however, preferred the adventures of Robinson Crusoe to the glories of ancient Greece and Rome and wrote in secret to his cousin John Flinders, then serving in the West Indies, to discover whether there was some chance of his entering naval service. His cousin offered him little hope, but encouraged him to study Robertson's *Elements of Navigation* and to make himself well acquainted with Moore's *Principles of Trigonometry,* rather than enter the service at a very young age.

To be an officer in the navy, although becoming more acceptable, was considered less gentlemanly than a commission in the army. At about that time the Napoleonic wars were giving the army a suitably elevated status, with commissioned rank having to be purchased at around £2,600. Where the army attracted the aristocracy, naval officers tended to be drawn from the ranks of the upper middle class or gentry. The second sons of landowners often went into the clergy, and it was not unusual, in turn, for the sons of clergy to go into the navy. Lord Nelson himself was the son of a clergyman, and was a good example of how a young boy who went to sea at the age of twelve could rise from the lowest rank to become one of history's immortal admirals. It was also a way for a young man of modest means to advance in society and to acquire wealth, particularly during times of war when bounties or prize moneys were given by the Admiralty for captured enemy vessels. No wonder it was much more exciting to become an army or naval officer than to be a clergyman, or a mere physician.

Matthew took the advice of his cousin in the West Indies, and before a year had passed he had so thoroughly mastered trigonometry and the practical science of navigation that he amazed his schoolmasters. He gave up all pretence of becoming a physician and at age sixteen, through the contacts of his cousin Henrietta, who was a governess to Captain Pasley's family, he presented himself as a volunteer aboard the *HMS Scipio.* Captain (later Admiral) Sir Thomas Pasley accepted Matthew as a lieutenant's servant and after a period transferred him to his

own ship, *HMS Bellerophon,* where Matthew served until the wars
with Spain waned.

Many years later, in her memoir, Ann Flinders was to record
the reason for Matthew's departure from his first patron after the
wars with Spain:

> *As our adventurer could never bear the thought of
> inactivity, in 1791 with the permission of his patron
> Captain Pasley, he embarked on board the* Providence,
> [. . . *on an expedition being fitted out under Captain, later
> Admiral Bligh, for the purpose of fetching the Breadfruit and
> other plants from the Friendly Islands . . .*] *from which time may
> be dated that passion for discovery, which never left
> him during life.*

Matthew Flinders' stepmother had a sister named Hannah who
had married Willingham Franklin (Hannah and Willingham were
the parents of the explorer Sir John Franklin, who was later to
accompany Flinders on the *Investigator*, and who still later, by a
strange convergence of destinies, became the Governor of
Tasmania). During their years in the family home at Donington,
the Flinders daughters, as well as son Matthew, became constant
companions of the neighbouring Franklin family. A great bond of
affection developed between the young Flinders and the Franklin
sisters, and when Matthew joined Captain Pasley, he wrote
frequently to his family and to the neighbouring Franklins,
addressing his letters always to his *'charming sisters'* with the
intention that they be read to all their friends.

Ann Chappelle was known to the Franklin sisters through the church, and we may surmise that she first heard of Matthew through the adventures he recounted to the *'charming sisters'* in his letters. When at last she did meet him she saw before her a young man three and a half years her junior. He was a good 7 inches taller than her, slight in appearance, of pale complexion, and with dark brown hair and eyes. Matthew began to write to her, too, but she was hesitant in answering, for although it was a popular pastime for young ladies to correspond regularly with relatives and friends, it was thought improper for an unmarried woman to write to a gentleman unless she was engaged to him.

2

Sea, I am thy servant

Matters of career called more strongly to Matthew than matters of the heart, and the young Flinders continued to pursue a life at sea, and to embark on the feats which wrote him forever into history. In an open boat just 33 feet long, with his friend the surgeon George Bass, he circumnavigated Tasmania, proving it was an island and opening up a shorter sea route from Britain. He was later to become the first known man to circumnavigate the island continent, which he called *'Terra Australis'* and afterwards recommended that it be called *'Australia'*. He discovered South Australia, charting the southern coast of the Great Australian Bight and the Spencer Gulf.

However, during his voyage on the *Norfolk* in 1798, the thought of Ann was sufficiently uppermost in Matthew's mind for him to name a smooth round hill in the Kent Group *'Mount Chappelle'*, and to call a nearby group of islands the *'Chappelle Islands'* (now spelt without the 'e').

At sea on 16th March 1799 — his twenty-fifth birthday — he wrote to Ann about the force which dominated his existence:

Sea, I am thy servant, but thy wages must afford me more than a bare subsistence. I do not mean to be always insulted. Thou art but a rough master, hast little mercy upon the lives and limbs of thy followers, but sometimes thou bestowest favours. Half my life I would dedicate to thee, but the whole I cannot if thou keepest me in penury all the morning and noon of life.

Six years after she had last seen him, now aged close to thirty and reconciled to spinsterhood, Ann was no longer the young woman Matthew had met before his journeying. She received a letter from him on his return to England while he was still on board the *Reliance* at the Nore.

Sept. 25, 1800

My dear friend

Have you received my letter of March 16 and Sept. 1, 1799, and another of Sept. 2, 1798? You answer yes? Then my dear friend the last letter which I have received from you is dated September 1797. If you think that I esteem you and value your friendship, it will be in your power to form a judgement of the uneasiness I have suffered on your account. From Thomas [Franklin] I learn that you are in the land of the living, and at present on a visit at Boston. My imagination has flown after you often and many a time, but the Lords of the Admiralty still keep me in confinement at the Nore. You must know, and your tender feelings have often anticipated for me, the rapturous pleasure I promised myself on returning from this Antipodean voyage, and an absence of six years.

As you are one of those friends whom I consider it indispensable and necessary to see, I should be glad to have some little account of your movements, where you reside and with whom; that my motions may be regulated accordingly. As soon as we shall be ordered up to Woolwich or to Deptford, which we expect daily, to be paid off, I shall go up to London occasionally to put the business I have got to do into fair training; and after the ship is paid off I shall reside there altogether till the principal part is executed; and this will properly take two months and more. But if the absence of people from London at this time should oblige me to defer some part till they return, then I shall take that opportunity of coming into Lincolnshire, if so long a time as three weeks can be spared.

You see that I make everything subservient to business. Indeed my dearest friend, this time seems to be a very critical period of my life. I have been long absent, have services abroad that were not expected, but which seem to be thought a good deal of. I have more and greater friends than before, and this seems to be the moment that their exertions may be the most serviceable to me. I may now perhaps make a bold dash forward, or remain a poor lieutenant all my life.

Although anxious to pursue his relationship with Ann, Matthew was, as he wrote to her, making '*everything subservient to business*'. In fact, just days before composing this letter he had written to his patron, Sir Joseph Banks, in the first of a series of exchanges which were to culminate in the young navigator's next voyage to Terra Australis:

> *This more minute examination of the coast . . . seems to point out, that . . . an extensive strait separates New South Wales from New Holland by the way of the Gulph of Carpentaria; or perhaps a southern gulph may only peninsulate New South Wales . . . It cannot be doubted, but that a very great part of that still extensive country remains either totally unknown, or has been partially examined at a time when navigation was much less advanced than at present. The interests of geography and natural history in general, and of the British nation in particular, seem to require, that this only remaining considerable part of the globe should be thoroughly explored.*

Well aware of the long and lonely periods of separation that friendship with Matthew would entail, Ann at first decided against answering his letter of 25th September. But Matthew had a young and ardent admirer in Isabella, who urged Ann to reply, and at her behest she did. (Isabella herself remained single all her life, and was thought by some to be more than half in love with Matthew but placing the happiness of her big sister first and foremost.)

A flurry of letters began between the two, their relationship progressing beyond mere friendship.

Ann at last asked Matthew whether his intentions were to settle down or to remain the wandering explorer. In reply, Matthew wrote of his hoped-for advancement in rank, and of the possibility of his travelling to Lincolnshire on Boxing Day with his patron. Then, in answer to her important question, he confessed that he must continue his work, that he must return to New South Wales:

> *Dec 18 1800*
> *16 Kay St*
> *Soho*

My dear friend,

I will begin by informing thee that a ship is fitting out for me to go out to New South Wales and this is to be ready, it is said, in the beginning of January. An astronomer and a naturalist are already engaged, and draftsmen are searching for. Everything seems to bespeak the utmost haste, but my appointment is not yet given out. The ship carries 20 guns at present and is called the Xenophon, *but she is to be rebaptised the* Investigator *and her guns reduced to 12.*

Let us then, my dear Annette, return to the 'sweet, calm delights of friendship'. Let us endeavour to return to that serenity of mind which thou possessed but lately.

I must call ambition to my assistance since it must be so; and in a life of activity and danger put out of my mind but that we are friends. The search after knowledge — the contemplation of nature in the barren world, the overlapping crags of utmost height and the open Fields decked with the spicy attire of the tropical climes may — nay must prevent me from casting one thought on England — on my home.

The ebullience of passions which come upon an ardent mind, which in solitude, have made me often vow that never would I return to New South Wales without a partner of my love. How are human projects blasted! But I will not any more indulge solitude. The human mind when unoccupied by business, does always indulge in scenes of fancied happiness. Mine shall always have employment.

Thus am I raising a barrier in imagination against the attacks of the common enemy of our peace. Approved thou of such a plan? If so, try it my dear friend . . .

And think not, my Annette, that I value thee less for the want of fortune. Heaven is my witness, that did I posses [sic] *ten thousand pounds tomorrow and I found thy person and mind what I think they are, my hand should await thy acceptance. Thou wilt write me once more so as to arrive before the 26th — of thy departure for Partney. By personal conferences we may be able to come to a better and more final understanding than by letter. Let us meet as lovers, and part as friends my Annette. Ah me!*

Brave words. Matthew did indeed follow them up with '*personal conferences*' for it appears he missed spending Christmas with his family, supposedly to be with Ann in Lincolnshire. However, their time together did not return them to the state of friendship that Matthew had envisaged, and he was to write to Ann next in an emotional state:

Jan 16 1801
16 King St, Soho

Excuse everything here, my dear dear friend — tears are in my eyes — I am torn to pieces.

Thou had promised to inform me when thou art married and I trust that the earliest opportunity afterwards will bring me the intelligence; it will be important to me. And whilst I am torn by winds and waves on various coasts and in various climes, may thou enjoy that serenity that a contemplative mind feels on surveying its own happiness. May thou meet with one whose mind and heart is worthy of thy love and whose circumstances unlike mine, can afford thee the enjoyment of life. Adieu, perhaps the last time. This excess of misery is too great to be often recalled. It is seldom that I have written a letter in tears.

Matt^w Flinders

Yet it was not adieu, for neither of them could walk away as easily as Matthew had proposed:

> *Investigator*
> *Sheerness*
> *27 Jan 1801*

> *My various occupations and provisions are at a stand; and to me there is no other being in the world than Annette. Thou, my dearest friend, hast not perhaps occupations that claim the whole of thy attention; fortunate indeed it is for me that I have; otherwise I had become the demonisation of fool, madman or villain 'ere this.*
>
> *Forget me Annette, put everything from thee that may recall forth recollections. However dear to me thy thoughts are, still is thy happiness dearer. But remember Annette — remember that I am thy friend. Banish every thing else from thee. On love I <u>must</u> not think; it has constituted the greatest happiness and the greatest misery of my life; but I will now <u>endeavour</u> to try what life is without it.*

Matthew had asked his father for a loan of £100 to set up a home so he could marry Ann, but his father believed the young Flinders should be capable of supporting himself, and rejected his request:

> *It cannot be any terrible task for a grown person in youth health and strength to obtain their own support . . . I well know it is a much harder one for a weak infirm father in*

the decline of life, to continue labouring for the whole to the
last hour of his earthly race.

Impetuously, Matthew wrote back to his father suggesting he think of himself as having only four children in the future.

Just over two months after their tearful decision that they could not and should not marry, Ann and Matthew faced the inevitability of the depth of their feelings for one another. A letter came from Matthew and, as was the custom, addressed to her via her stepfather, so that it could be read to ensure its propriety. It was a difficult medium through which to write love letters.

H.M.S. Investigator at the Nore
April 6. 1801

My dearest friend

Thou has asked me if there is a <u>possibility</u> of our living together. I think I see a <u>probability</u> of living with a moderate share of comfort. Till now, I was not certain of being able to fit myself out clear of the world. I have now done it; and have accommodation on board the Investigator, *in which as my wife, a woman may, with <u>love</u> to assist her, make herself happy. This prospect has recalled all the tenderness which I have so reluctantly endeavoured to banish. I am sent for to London, where I shall be from the 9th to the 19th or perhaps longer. If thou wilt meet me there, this hand shall be thine forever.*

If thou has sufficient love and courage, say to Mr and Mrs Tyler, that I require nothing more with thee than a sufficient stock of clothes, and a small sum to answer the increased expenses that will necessarily and immediately come upon me; as such for living on board, as providing for at Port Jackson; for whilst I am employed in the most dangerous part of my duty, thou shalt be placed under some friendly roof there. I will specify this sum to be £200, or if great inconvenience will result from advancing it, I will say £150; and I leave every thing future to the justice and generosity of thy parents and friends.

It is but a bad specimen of my stability to change in this manner, as appearances will bespeak I do; but it is no change. It is only just now that I see attendant comfort; the want of which only kept me back.

I need not, or at this time have I time to enter into a detail of my income and prospects; it will, I trust, be sufficient for me to say that I see a fortune growing under me, to meet increasing expenses. I only want to have a fair start, and my life for it we will do well, and be happy. I will write further tomorrow; but shall most anxiously expect thy answer at 26 Fleet St London on my arrival on Friday; and I trust thy presence immediately afterwards. Mr or perhaps Mrs Tyler will most probably accompany thee. I have only time to add, that most anxiously I am

most sincerely thine,
Matt^w Flinders

It will be much better to keep this matter entirely secret.
There are many reasons for it yet, and I have also a
powerful one. I do not exactly know how my great friends
might like it.

Ann's stepfather, taking sympathy on the pair, offered them
financial support. Marriage was very much a family concern, and
fathers, brothers and cousins were responsible for the wellbeing
and livelihood of unmarried female family members, so the
Reverend Tyler's gift, though indeed generous, was probably also
based on practical financial considerations.

The wars with France had produced high inflation, and the
cost of maintaining households and landholdings continued to
greatly increase. This had diminished the fortunes of many, yet
vastly increased the wealth of others, and it was normal for
parents in these turbulent times to place a high importance on
money. Young people were expected to respect their parents'
wishes on the suitability of a marriage partner. If love or affection
was part of that equation, then everyone was the happier.
However, matters of high finance and dowries of substance did
not greatly affect Matthew and Ann, for neither side was able to
offer anything more than the means to live adequately. Theirs was
most definitely a love match.

For once in Matthew's life, time and good fortune coincided. In
addition to the financial help which the Reverend Tyler offered,
Matthew was also able to sell the real estate he had purchased in
Banks Town on his voyage to New South Wales to a Mr Bowles
for £300. (The land, alongside that of George Bass, fronted

Prospect Creek just off Georges River, in what is now Georges Hall. It is still identifiable by Flinders Avenue and Flinders Slopes, and is close by Bankstown Airport.)

Then, to cap this good fortune, the Admiralty offered him the command of the *Investigator* to sail to the colony on a voyage of exploration, '*the pursery of which had added to my situation, so that a moderate computation made £300 or £400 a year on which a wife could be kept genteelly,*' Flinders wrote in his journal that year. With their increased opportunities for financial security, and knowing his career prospects were about to be enhanced, the couple thought more about a life together, yet knew too that Matthew would soon sail away.

Even before their marriage Ann recognised the strength and perseverance within him, and loved him for it. Ann's prophetic words to her friend Fanny at the time were long to haunt her: '*I don't admire want of firmness in a man. I love courage and determination in the male character.*'

3

Never a man more happy

The course of true love continued to be storm-tossed, with the precarious nature of their financial status, the responsibilities of marriage, and the prospect of a long separation continuing to weigh heavily on both Ann and Matthew. Just weeks before the wedding, Matthew wrote to his father that he and Miss Chappelle had had an attachment but had tried to wean themselves of it: '*I have no present or future intention of marrying either her or any other person, but leave England only wedded to my ship.*' Yet on 3rd April, aboard the *Investigator*, Matthew wrote his last will and testament, marriage or no marriage. He wished half of his estate to pass to Miss Chappelle '*as a proof of my sincere regard*'. Ten days after the aforementioned letter, Dr Flinders received another informing him that his son and Ann Chappelle intended marrying immediately, and that Matthew planned to take her with him on the voyage to Terra Australis. In fact his determination to take Ann on board the *Investigator* to the colony of New South Wales appears to have been the deciding factor in their decision to marry. There were precedents for a commander to travel with his wife and Matthew had decided to take her on board, to install her in his cabin, aware always that he did not know how his important friends might like it.

Matthew Flinders was a man torn between competing longings. He was obsessed with achieving his place in history through feats of discovery and navigation in the manner of his hero Captain James Cook. He was also a man deeply in love. His dilemma was that Flinders the naval officer believed, with some justification, that marriage would lessen his chance of selection by the Lords of the Admiralty to command the voyage of discovery to Terra Australis. There were other unmarried officers ready and able to step into this role.

However, even flawed solutions are the torch-bearers of hope, and he resolved to marry Ann and take her on board the *Investigator* in secret.

On Friday 17th April 1801 the two were married in St Nicholas Church in Partney, the village in which the Tylers lived. The Reverend Tyler read the wedding service himself, and the couple were married by a licence most probably granted by the bishop. Hannah Franklin and Mary Hudson signed the marriage register as witnesses to the solemnisation of the union. It was a bright spring day, the daffodils bloomed in the fields, and pink-blossomed trees bowed under their floral offerings, carpeting the pathways. In stark contrast the old stone church, the focal point of so many village activities, stood sombrely amidst its grey crumbling tombstones and oak tree sentinels, ancient even then. Isabella, at sixteen years of age, described the groom as:

This Marriage was solemnized between Us {

in the Presence of { Wm Fletcher
Two O'Ople

Frances Frith
Faith Flanders

were

N° 34 } Matthew Flinders Cumming Bachelor of this Parish
Royal Navy & Ann Chappell of this Parish

Married in this Church by Licence

this seventeenth Day of April in the Year One Thousand eight Hundred

and one

By me Wm Tyler Rector of Brayton

Matthew Flinders

This Marriage was solemnized between Us { Ann Chappelle

in the Presence of { Hannah Chappelle
Mary Hudson

Detail of Ann and Matthew's marriage certificate

Never a man more happy than poor Matthew and he determined to be so, in spite of the Lords of the Admiralty and Sir Joseph Banks. Yes of all the merry group none more merry than he.

In the end Ann and Matthew's wedding had been hastily arranged to coincide with his shore leave. Matthew had scarcely had time to send a letter to Ann telling her he could take just five days' leave the following week and that they could be married with her family in attendance in Partney instead of in London. He caught the evening coach and through the night his restless thoughts were already on the future — his wife, their life together, the reaction of the Admiralty when they discovered his plans. He had little thought for the towns the coach passed through, the slow meal stops, the beauty of the countryside, the daffodils in bloom. He wrote to his cousin Henrietta in April 1801 about the wedding day:

Everything was agreed to in a very handsome manner, and just at this time I was called up to town and found that I might be spared a few days from thence. I set off on Wednesday evening from town, arrived next evening at Spilsby, was married next morning, which was Friday; on Saturday we went to Donington, on Sunday reached Huntingdon, and on Monday were in town. Next morning I presented myself before Sir Joseph Banks with a grave face as if nothing had happened, and then went on with my business as usual. We stayed in town till the following Sunday, and came on board the Investigator *next day, and here we have remained ever since, a few weeks on shore and a day spent on the Essex side of the Thames excepted.*

Honeymoons were not yet the custom of the day, and it is likely that Ann may have been accompanied home by Isabella after the wedding. The Reverend Tyler made good his promise of a dowry for Ann, giving Matthew a roll of banknotes which the groom placed in his boot for safekeeping.

The following day the newlyweds journeyed to Donington to see Matthew's father. They stayed one night and Dr Flinders was said to have felt great unease, writing in his diary:

With concern note that my Son Matt^r came upon us suddenly & unexpectedly with a Wife on Sat. April 18 & left us next day — it is a Miss Chapple of Partney. We had known of the acquaintance, but had no Idea of Marriage taking place until the completion of his ensuing Voyage. I wish he may not repent his hasty step.

Matthew was to refer to his father's reaction in a letter to Ann some years later:

I acknowledge myself not having been pleased [with the marriage of his sister Elizabeth] *... The idea that young girls are at liberty to marry whom they please without consulting any of their friends, may do much harm in society, and should be opposed. She may say* *that if she married without her father's consent, so did I but independently of the difference between a man of 28 and a young woman of 22, perhaps she did not know, when I spoke to my father of my affection to thee, he acknowledge thou wert a most worthy young lady from all that he knew and . . . it was under the circumstances relating to my voyage which allowed me no time to take the advice of friends.*

In the belief that she would soon be sailing with Matthew to New South Wales, Ann wrote hurriedly to inform her friend Elizabeth Flinders, Matthew's sister, of their marriage:

April 17th 1801.

My beloved Betsy,

Thou wilt be much surprised to hear of this sudden affair; indeed I scarce believe it myself, tho' I have this very morning given my hand at the altar to him I have ever highly esteemed, and it affords me no small pleasure that I am now part, tho' a distant one, of thy family, my Betsy. It grieves me much thou art so distant from me. Thy society would have greatly cheered me. Thou wilt to-day pardon me if I say but little. I am scarce able to coin one sentence or to write intelligibly. It pains me to agony when I indulge the thought for a moment that I must leave all I value on earth, save one, alas, perhaps for ever. Ah, my Betsy, but

I dare not, must not, think. Therefore, farewell, farewell. May the great God of Heaven preserve thee and those thou lovest, oh, everlastingly. Adieu, dear darling girl; love as ever, though absent and far removed, from your poor

Annette

In April 1801, the month of their marriage, Matthew Flinders wrote of his impending voyage to Terra Australis:

my greatest ambition is to make such a minute investigation of this extensive and very interesting country that no person shall have occasion to come after me to make further discoveries.

Sir Joseph Banks wrote to him on the *Investigator*:

with sincere good wishes for your future prosperity, and with a firm belief that you will, in your future conduct, do credit to yourself as an able investigator, and to me as having recommended you.

But for the untimely visit of the commissioners of the Admiralty to the ship, the newlyweds would have sailed safely to Port Jackson, where Flinders' intention was to leave Ann with a reputable family while he undertook the more hazardous and uncharted portions of his journeys, and then to bring her home again to England.

However, the Lords of the Admiralty were informed that Mrs Flinders was observed seated '*in the captain's cabin without her bonnet*'. The first Matthew heard of their horror at such a sight was in a letter from Banks, who wrote on 21st May:

> . . . *news of your marriage, which was published in the Lincoln paper, has reached me. The Lords of the Admiralty have heard also that Mrs Flinders is on board the* Investigator, *and that you have some thought of carrying her to sea with you. This I was very sorry to hear, and if that is the case I beg to give you my advice by no means to adventure to measures so contrary to the regulations and the discipline of the Navy; for I am convinced by language I have heard, that their Lordships will, if they hear of her being in New South Wales, immediately order you to be supersed, whatever may be the consequences, and in all likelihood order Mr Grant to finish the survey.*

Firm and determined, though perhaps not in a way that was immediately appreciated by the distraught new bride, Flinders wrote immediately to Banks. It must have been a letter which caused great anguish for both Ann and Matthew, but the idea of being parted would have given rise to unbelievable dismay for Ann. She had resisted even writing to him in the early days of their friendship because she so dreaded the prospect of months of lonely separation while he was at sea in unknown oceans, in unknown circumstances.

Matthew wrote:

> *I am much indebted to you, Sir Joseph, for the information
> contained in your letter of the 21st. It is true that I had an
> intention of taking Mrs Flinders to Port Jackson, to
> remain there until I should have completed the voyage, and
> to have then brought her home again in the ship, and I trust
> that the service would not have suffered in the least by such
> a step. The Admiralty have most probably conceived that I
> intended to keep her on board during the voyage, but this
> was far from my intentions . . . If their Lordships
> understood this matter in its true light, I should hope that
> they would have shown the same indulgence to me as to
> Lieut. Kent of the* Buffalo, *and many others . . . If their
> Lordships' sentiments should continue the same, whatever
> may be my disappointment, I shall give up the wife for the
> voyage of discovery; and I would beg of you, Sir Joseph, to
> be assured that even this circumstance will not damp the
> ardour I feel to accomplish the important purpose of the
> present voyage, and in a way that shall preclude the
> necessity of any one following after me to explore.*

A few days later Flinders wrote again to Banks to ensure there was
no misunderstanding in the representation Banks would make on
his behalf to the Lords of the Admiralty:

> *I foresee that, although I should in the case of Mrs
> Flinders going to Port Jackson have been more particularly*

cautious of my stay there, yet their Lordships will conclude naturally enough that her presence would tend to increase the number of and to lengthen my visits. I am therefore afraid to risk their Lordships' ill opinion, and Mrs Flinders will return to her friends immediately that our sailing orders arrive.

In reply Banks wrote:

I yesterday went to the Admiralty to enquire about the Investigator, *and was indeed much mortified to learn there that you had been on shore in Hythe Bay, and I was still more mortified to hear that several of your men had deserted, and that you had had a prisoner entrusted to your charge, who got away at a time when the quarter-deck was in charge of a midshipman. I heard with pain many severe remarks on these matters, and in defence I could only say that as Captain Flinders is a sensible man and a good seaman, such matters could only be attributed to the laxity of discipline which always takes place when the captain's wife is on board, and that such lax discipline could never again take place, because you had wisely resolved to leave Mrs Flinders with her relations.*

The truth of these desertions was that in preparing to leave the Nore on 25th May, Flinders had recalled a party of fifteen of his men who had been lent to the *Advice* to work on her brig. Only twelve of the fifteen returned, the others having vanished. There was little Matthew could have done. However, the Admiralty, like Banks, was not pleased.

The next day, just five days after Banks' first letter of warning to him, Flinders left the Nore — at the mouth of the Thames — for Spithead — at Portsmouth — to await his sailing orders. He had no master on board to act as pilot but Flinders was an experienced navigator, and they were still in home waters. As he did not yet have orders to commence his voyage proper, he took his bride of five weeks with him, and even in that short distance she suffered greatly from the motion of the seas. Fate seemed to be running against Flinders, for just two days and only 3 or 4 miles from shore, and still in familiar waters, the *Investigator* wedged onto an uncharted bank. The vessel was unharmed and was later able to resume her journey. Where others may have left the incident unreported, Flinders, the dedicated navigator and chartmaker, considered it his duty to seek to amend the Admiralty chart to save other vessels from going aground in less calm seas. Sir Joseph Banks reported to his protégé that the Lords were sorely displeased with Flinders. It was their opinion that the *Investigator* had struck the sandbank solely because Mrs Flinders was on board and possibly distracting the commander of the vessel.

It was no wonder the Lords of the Admiralty were sensitive to women on board at that time for one of their own heroes, the then Vice-Admiral Lord Nelson, was scandalising society by his association with Lady Emma Hamilton, a married woman whom he escorted onto his ships from time to time. Lady Hamilton's influence over him was considered so great that she was widely regarded as the reason Nelson disobeyed orders to leave Naples (where Lady Hamilton lived with her husband) to join a squadron in the Mediterranean.

Ann and Matthew's new-found happiness together served only to deepen the wound of their impending separation, but both reluctantly accepted its necessity. The practical side of Ann understood the compelling ambition which drove her new husband; the emotional side did not. Although Matthew was employed in a task which was also his life's passion, he knew that he would have to sail the oceans if he were to support a wife financially.

Before the *Investigator* sailed from the Nore, Matthew confessed to a friend:

> *It is certain, I should not have married but with the idea of taking her with me, others had been allowed this privilege and I could not foresee that I should not have been denied it . . . Yet I am by no means sorry for having married. If you knew her worth you would not.*

4

Thy own wanderer

Matthew's difficult but inevitable decision to comply with Admiralty wishes distressed Ann so deeply that friends, fearful for her health, took her to London to be comforted and cared for. Not only did she face many months, if not years, without him, there was always the likelihood that she might never see him again, for he was sailing into largely unexplored and uncharted waters. From her point of view, he faced not a voyage of great discovery but the possibility of shipwreck many months from any hope of rescue and perhaps with a lingering death. He faced a lack of hygiene, a lack of adequate food and water, and like his former commander Bligh, perhaps even the prospect of a hostile crew who might revolt against the harsh conditions of shipboard life.

Had Ann been allowed to remain on board the *Investigator*, Matthew felt he would have been sailing not only with a wife, but with a true and close friend. He wrote to his father from Spithead, *'I find her so much superior in penetration and judgement to the generality of women, that there are but few occurrences upon which I do not consult her.'*

His true friend and companion, however, was sick at heart and sick in health at the thought of his impending departure.

Matthew wrote to Ann:

Investigator
Spithead
July 5, 1801

I trust that a very short period indeed will now see me absent from England and each wasting day will then bring nearer the period of my return. Rest confident, my dear, of thy ardent and unalterable affection of thy own MF; he <u>does</u> love thee beyond everything. I go, beloved, to gather riches and laurels with which to adorn thee; rejoice at the opportunity which fortune and circumstances give me to do it. Rest assured of the unalterable affection of <u>thy own</u> wanderer.

MF

Ann and Matthew wrote almost daily to each other.

To Mrs Flinders, Battersea — Spithead July 12 1801

I have not yet got thy letter today, my dearest girl, but I must be writing to thee. Thou thinkest of going tomorrow or Thursday into Lincolnshire. Although I have so much wished for thee to be with thy mother, I yet feel that I am sorry at the increase of our distance, and more especially since I see no prospect of getting my sailing orders. What thinkest thou then, if I should remain another month or two waiting as I have been, thou be in the country, so many miles from me? and in health! I cannot bear the idea.

Does thy eye and thy strength enable thee to travel to Peterborough by thyself, or does Mr Tyler come for thee? If Mr T does come, thou wilt go down comfortably. But if he does not, perhaps thou wouldst be as well able to travel to Portsmouth as to Peterborough. But are the clothes thou hast with thee sufficient for a stay of a month or two? If thou couldst manage in this particular, and Mr Tyler does not come up to town! What shall I say? I will only say that I will intirely leave thee to take that course that, every circumstance being considered, thou shalt judge best; but remember, my best love, to take into the consideration, the possibility or probability of a relapse to thy former state of health, arising either from the fatigue of a days travelling or otherwise. If thou judgest from thy present state of health that there is a <u>probability</u> then we must not risk thy constitution, and having to come over again all the routine of misery thou hast once undergone. I will not express a wish either way, for thou canst not but please me. By considering thy health thou will consult my happiness, oh most closely; thou wilt shew thy affection to extend to periods of longer duration than the present moments. By coming here thou wilt also convince me of thy affection, if I wanted such a proof. I can therefore only add on this subject, that if thou goest into Lincolnshire, which must be the case if Mr T *comes up . . . then I do not know of anything further that remains for me to do for thee. If thou comest here, thou wilt find the Portsmouth coaches at the Golden Cross, from the Angel at the back of St Clements and at the Spread Eagle or Cross Keys (I forget which) in Gracechurch St. Mr Hippins will secure thee a place, and thou must then write saying when thou shalt set off, and whether thou comest to Portsmouth or Gosport: if the former, desire to be set down at the Crown where I will be. Shouldst thou prefer to live on board, I will get a feather bed for thy poor joints; if on shore I will get a <u>snug room</u>, somewhere on the Gosport side, and be with thee, and <u>love thee</u> as much as I can.*

I ernestly beg of thee not even <u>to think</u> which of the above plans will please me best, but which will please [thee].

Ann did not return to Spithead, her distressed state being such that she was accompanied home to her family in Lincolnshire. Long before he sailed, Matthew missed her deeply. He wrote to her in June:

I am just as awkward without thee as one half of a pair of scissors without its fellow . . . The idea of how happy we might be will sometimes intrude itself and take away the little spirits that thy melancholy situation leaves me . . . thou dearest, kindest, best of women.

The *Investigator* sailed on 17th July, three months to the day after their marriage.

Exacerbating their separation was the irregularity and unreliability of mail, for letters could only hope to catch up with Matthew in far ports, not only where he was scheduled to call, but also at times which coincided with his visits. The Admiralty's Naval Transport Office was the main international postal service available to the families of British seamen. In December, five months after sailing, and with no hope yet of having received a letter from Ann, Matthew implored her:

> *Write to me constantly; write me pages and volumes. Tell me the dress thou wearest, tell me thy dreams, anything, so do but talk to me and of thyself. When though art sitting at thy needle and alone, then think of me, my love, and write me the uppermost of thy thoughts. Fill me half a dozen sheets, and send them when thou canst. Think only, my dearest girl upon the gratification which the perusal and reperusal fifty times repeated will afford me, and thou will write me something or other every day. Adieu, my dearest, best love.*

Although Ann destroyed her own letters to her husband, considering them too personal for others to read after her death, his were too precious to dispose of, even at the risk of others reading them at some later date. (Little could she have imagined that, in Britain and Australia at least, generations would continue to read his letters of longing to her for centuries to come.)

Ann did not immediately write to Matthew, and when he did not hear from her, he wrote with a sense of dejection:

A moment snatched from the confusion of performing half-a-dozen occupations . . . is a poor tribute to offer to a beloved friend like thee. That I am safe and well, and have done everything thus far that I could have expected to do, is to tell thee something. How highly should I value such short information reciprocated from thee! But alas, my dearest love, I am all in the dark concerning thee, I know not what to fear or what to hope.

It was not until 1802 that Matthew was to hear from Ann, after a year filled with yearning for his new wife and worry for her wellbeing. Then he received two letters, one dated October 1801, the other 7th January 1802, in which she wrote of an illness which had necessitated an operation to save her sight. Excessive weeping was said to have caused severe inflammation in her eye. Alone and distressed at the loss of her husband to The New World, Ann had endless time to dwell on her anguish, to question her decision to marry, and to all but drown in the pain of her sorrow. She despaired that Matthew truly loved her.

He wrote immediately:

My dearest love,

. . . Oh my love, my love, how much do I sympathise in thy sufferings, that could I but transport myself to thee and with thee whilst thou should rest upon my fond bosom; thee wouldst then know that my heart beats with such rapidity as it ever could have done, for thee.

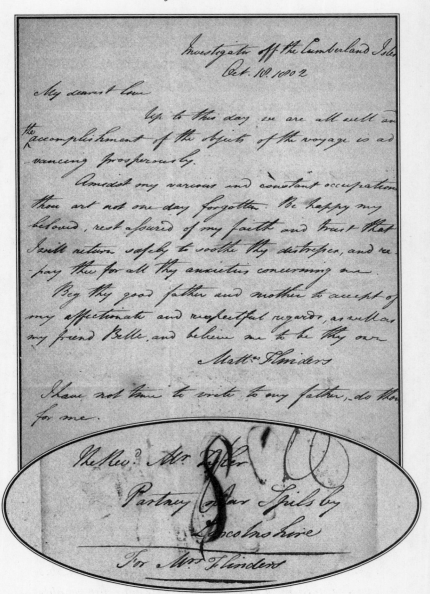

Investigator off the Cumberland Isles
Oct. 10. 1802

My dearest love

Up to this day we are all well and the accomplishment of the objects of the voyage is advancing prosperously.

Amidst my various and constant occupations thou art not one day forgotten. Be happy my beloved, rest assured of my faith and trust that I will return safely to soothe thy distresses, and repay thee for all thy anxieties concerning me.

Beg thy good father and mother to accept of my affectionate and respectful regards, as well as my friend Belle, and believe me to be thy own

Matt* Flinders

I have not time to write to my father,—do thou for me.

The Revᵈ. Mr Tyler
Partney near Spilsby
Lincolnshire

For Mr* Flinders

Matthew's heartfelt letter-writing

My dearest friend, thou adducest my leaving thee to follow the call of my profession, as a poor proof of my affection for thee. Dost thou not know, my beloved, that we could have barely existed in England? That both thou and me must have been debarred of even necessaries; unless we had given up our independence to have procured them from perhaps unwilling friends. It was only upon the certainty of obtaining an employment, the produce of which would be adequate to thy support as well as my own, that I dared to follow the wishes of my heart and press thee to be mine. Heaven knows with what sincerity and warmth of affection I have loved thee, — how anxiously I look forward to the time when I may return to thee, and how earnestly I labour that the delight of our meeting may be no more clouded with the fear of a long parting. Do not then, my beloved, adduce the following of the dictates of necessity as my crime. Rather, my dearest Ann, let us submit to what has been deemed for us and look forward with our best hopes for the good which is in store for us . . . Let not unavailing sorrow increase thy malady, but look my dear Ann to the happy side. See me engaged, successfully thus far, in the cause of science and followed by the good wishes and approbation of the world . . . hastening to thy love as the best reward for all my toils.

At least for him their separation was salved by the rewards of a work in which he was supremely satisfied. While Ann waited alone in England, Matthew's reputation as the outstanding navigator of his time was being established. It was left to Ann to help her mother around the house. She lived with her mother, stepfather and half-sister in a household she could not furnish or claim as her own, no matter how much she was loved within its walls. Each passing year narrowed the prospect of children and a family of her own while around her, friends' children grew and were joined by newer siblings. Spouses lived their days together in contented domesticity, leading blissfully ordinary lives.

After another long year of no news from home, twelve months' worth of letters awaited Matthew on his arrival in Port Jackson in 1803. Within them was the news of the death of his father more than a year earlier. Filled with remorse that he had not reconciled with his father before his death, Matthew wrote to his mother:

> *The death of so kind a father and who was so excellent a man is a heavy blow, and strikes deep into my heart. The duty I owed him, and which I had now a prospect of paying with the warmest affection and gratitude, had made me look forward to the time of our return with increased ardour ... O, my dearest, kindest father, how much I loved and revered you, you cannot now know.*

He wrote to Ann with news, and love, as well as the precariousness of life and the proximity of death, but it would be almost as long again for his letters to reach her. His letter did little to reassure Ann that she would ever see him again:

Port Jackson, June 25, 1803

Grateful for thy recovered health, my dearest love, and grateful to thee for thy many and long and most dear remembrances of me, which I have received on our arrival here some days since. How shall I express the anguish of my heart at the dreadful havock that death is making all around. How dear is the name of father to an affectionate son, and how sweet [was] *the idea of being soon able to console and assist him in his every want and wish. When parting, with the hope of soon shewing that my actions should prove better than my words how much I loved him, how dreadful is this blow. Tis too painful for me to be dwelt upon, although, alas, I have lately had too much experience of death's power, for my eyes cannot scarcely be turned where some victim does not die. Douglas — the boatswain is gone, the sargeant, two quarter masters and another followed before we got into this port; and since, the gardener, and three others are laid in earth. Death's hand is now staid, and his envious eye which had been cast upon more of us seems to be turning away.*

But little indeed can be boasted of our state and condition, but thou shalt have some brief account of us; and first — of the ship;— A survey has been held upon her and which proves her to be so very much decayed as to be totally irreparable. It was the unanimous opinion of the surveying officers that had we met a severe gale of wind in the passage from Timor that she must have been crushed like an egg and gone down. I was partly aware of her bad

42

state, and returned sooner to Port Jackson, before the worst weather came, on that account. For me, whom this obstruction in the voyage, and the melancholy state of my poor people have much distressed, I have been lame about four months and was much debilitated in health, and I fear in constitution, but am now recovering and shall soon be altogether well ... *Trim* [the cat], *like his master is becoming grey; he is at present fat and frisky, and takes meat from our forks with his former dexterity: he is commonly my bedfellow ...*

... As I shall be better ably in a few weeks to say how the voyage will be prosecuted, and how soon we may probably return, I will leave Port Jackson and return to thy dear and kind letter I have now before me — the following two dated in December 1801 — one in January 1802 — and another in February, June and September 1802. All these I found on our arrival, and for which I am most grateful to thee, and also to thy father and mother for their enclosures. Thou has shewn me how very ill I have requited thy tender love in several cases. I cannot excuse myself now, but plead for respite until my return when in thy dear arms I will beg for pardon and if thou cannot forgive me all, will have it sealed with ten thousand kisses. If I could laugh at the effusions of thy tenderness, it would be to me the idolatrous language thou frequently usest to me. Thou makest an idol, and then worshippest it; and like some of the inhabitants of the east, thou also bestoweth a little occasional castigation, just to let the ugly *deity know the value of thy devotion. Thinkest though not my dearest love that I shall be spoiled by thy endearing flatteries? I fear it, and yet can hardly part with one, so dear to me is thy affection in whatever way expressed:*

I cannot allow that my love is far behind thine, I am indeed far behind thee in expressing affection. Measure me not by this but believe, my dearest and only love, that very, very often my thoughts which are never expressed, are devoted to thee. In torture at thy great distance from me, I lay musing upon thee and whilst sighs of fervent love, compassion for thy suffering health, and admiration of thy excellencies in turn get utterance . . . my heart is with thee, and so soon as I can insure for us a moderate portion of the comforts of life, thou wilt see whether love or ambition have the greater power over me.

Before thou was mine, I had engaged in this voyage; — without it we could not live. Thou knowst not the struggle in my bosom, before I consented to the necessity. There was no prospect of a permanent subsistence but in pursuing what I had undertaken, and I doubt not but that it will answer the end.

5

A safe and expeditious voyage?

In Sydney, with the *Investigator* decayed beyond use, Governor King offered Flinders the little *Lady Nelson* among a number of other vessels, but all were inadequate for the surveying task and long journey ahead. The armed ship *HMS Porpoise* was decided upon as the best available, although it, too, was far from sound.

Although Flinders had earlier successfully combined command of a ship with his intensive duties of chartmaking, Governor King gave command of the *Porpoise* to a junior officer, Robert Fowler, so that Flinders could concentrate on his surveying. In the company of two other ships, the little *Porpoise* headed north.

The dangers of seafaring life that Ann feared for Matthew were all too real, for just seven nights out of Sydney, the officer of the watch on *Porpoise* saw waves breaking ahead and called urgently to Fowler. He tried wretchedly to steer the ship to safety while Flinders, below decks, was unaware of the imminent danger. As he was not the commanding officer

Flinders was not called to the bridge though he was of course well experienced in command and in navigation. Neither the *Porpoise* nor the accompanying *Cato* were able to avert disaster, both striking the reef. The third ship, the *Bridgewater*, cleared the danger and after standing by for several hours, continued on its way — perhaps thinking all hands were lost, perhaps not wanting to risk shipwreck itself. (Whatever the captain's reasoning, he saw fit to tell quite a different version of events to those of the survivors when at last he reported the accident.) The *Cato* was torn apart and its planks washed away. The *Porpoise* was slightly more fortunate, and at dawn Flinders, taking command of the survivors' plight, climbed as high as he could on the damaged vessel to survey their proximity to land. A dry sandbank was seen above high-water mark, and Flinders gave orders for the crews of both ships to make to safety. In the light of day it was clear that the *Bridgewater* could have rescued the crews with little risk to its own safety.

Ninety-four men were stranded almost 730 miles from port and well out from the mainland, but fortunately with three months' provisions. A makeshift settlement was established and then Flinders — with one other officer, a crew of twelve rowers and three weeks' provisions — set out for Port Jackson and rescue. Three weeks later, when they were at the end of their rations, Governor King received news of their plight with tears in his eyes. A rescue vessel was dispatched immediately, and six weeks after Flinders had left the stranded men, he stepped ashore once more to the cheers and shouts of the survivors. Flinders himself wrote of the experience, '*the pleasure of rejoining my companions so amply provided with the means of relieving their distress made this one of the happiest moments of my life.*' The spot, off Mackay in Queensland, was henceforth known as Wreck Reef.

Safely back in Port Jackson, plans were made for Flinders to take command of the *Cumberland* for the return journey to England. *The Sydney Gazette* proudly proclaimed that Flinders and his crew were to command '*the first Vessel built in the Colony to England — May her Voyage be safe and expeditious!*' Such was the condition of ships in the colony, however, that the *Cumberland*, too, was beset with problems. From the beginning of the voyage it leaked to a greater extent than had been anticipated. The condition of the pumps went from bad to worse with constant and excessive use, and there was a strong chance that in heavy seas the ship would capsize or sink, taking all with her.

Matthew's decision to persevere in the *Cumberland* may well have been the worst decision he made in his career. It was certainly to have disastrous consequences.

The ship called at Timor for provisions and makeshift repairs, then set sail for the Cape of Good Hope. Three weeks after leaving land, the vessel was in serious danger of foundering. It was far from home and far from rescue, and Flinders was forced to consider changing course to repair the ship and to refit the rattling, shaking, ineffective pumps. Even at night the pumps could no longer be rested, for just an hour and a half without pumping meant the men were ankle deep in water. Flinders and his men listened constantly for any change to the laboured heartbeat of the machine on which all their lives now depended.

It was not only the leaks that plagued the crew, for the *Cumberland* was difficult to manoeuvre, and uncomfortable in many ways. Flinders wrote:

> *Of all the filthy little things I ever saw, this schooner, for bugs, lice, fleas, weavels, mosquitos, cockroaches large and small, and mice, rises superior to them all. We have almost got the better of the fleas, lice and mosquitos, but in spite of boiling water and the daily destruction amongst them, the bugs still keep their ground. I have never stripped myself before the last two nights, but usually slept upon the lee locker with my clothes on; notwithstanding which I have at least a hundred lumps upon my body and arms; and before this vile bug-like smell will leave me, must, I believe, as well as my clothes, undergo a good boiling in the large kettle.*

When he had sailed from Port Jackson, Flinders was of the belief that there was still peace between England and France although there was always the possibility of war. Should he try to make it to the Cape? He had a passport of safe passage from the French Government but not the Dutch (who were also likely to be at war with England). At that time, however, passports were issued in the name of a ship, and Flinders had had to change from the unseaworthy *Investigator*, in whose name the passport was issued, to the leaky *Cumberland*. He considered Île de France as the lesser of two evils, particularly as the French had always looked favourably upon geographic research voyages. He had no charts of the Île de France, but a description in the third edition of the *Encyclopaedia*

Britannica, which Matthew carried on board, indicated the principal harbour, Port Louis, lay on the north-western side of the island.

At noon on 15th December, as they neared land a small French schooner was seen near the shore. Flinders steered in her wake, thinking it fortunate to be able to follow a vessel which knew the local shoals and currents. However, the captain of the small vessel thought he was being pursued by a British warship and made for the safety of the harbour at Cape Bay, where troops with muskets appeared as soon as word from the schooner reached them. Flinders concluded that England and France were at war and sent an officer ashore to communicate their benign intentions. All appeared to be soon resolved and the senior officer in the port invited Flinders to dine with him. Still, the fact that the passport had been issued in the name of another ship was a discrepancy which required the personal attention of the Governor in Port Louis. So the next day, accompanied by the local senior officer, the *Cumberland* sailed to Port Louis and the Governor, General De Caen.

The General was a short-tempered man and his manner was brusque in dealing with this English commander. He was sceptical that a voyage of exploration would set forth in a tiny 29-ton vessel and expressed himself dissatisfied with Flinders' answers and the business he claimed to be upon. De Caen then ordered an officer and an interpreter to accompany Flinders on board the *Cumberland,* where they demanded the ship's papers, charts and books relating to Flinders' voyage of discovery, as well as any letters and packets of mail which might be on board. The documents were all placed in a trunk, which was lashed closed then sealed by Flinders before being taken ashore to the Governor's house.

6

I sought protection and have found a prison

Flinders and Aken, his second-in-command, were taken ashore at one o'clock in the morning and a guard left on the *Cumberland*. They were taken to a '*tavern*' with a surprisingly prison-like appearance and a soldier placed at their door. The following day Flinders was taken before an English-speaking officer and questioned at length about the discrepancy in his passport, why he chased a vessel in sight of land, and what induced him to put into port. Flinders' answers were all recorded, to be translated into French for the General. During the course of the questioning, when Flinders tabled a letter from Governor King relating to the *Cumberland,* he at last began to sense a change in attitude by his questioners. At about five o'clock Flinders was handed an invitation from the General to dine with him and his wife, something which Flinders decided he would decline until such time as he was set at liberty. A close colleague of De Caen was later to write from the General's perspective that Flinders was received by De Caen who was '*in uniform, the head uncovered* [but] *Captain Flinders presented himself with arrogance, his hat upon his head; they had to ask him to remove it.*' Flinders' lack of respect for a senior officer and his lack of politeness in declining the dinner invitation were enough for the short-tempered De Caen to detain Flinders while he reported him to Paris. It was a detention that was to continue for six and a half years. It was a lesson in humility and tact that would be learnt by Flinders in the harshest manner.

He later wrote to Ann:

I shall learn patience in this island, which will perhaps counteract the insolence acquired by having had unlimited command over my fellow men. You know, my dearest, that I always dreaded the effect that the possession of great authority would have upon my temper and disposition. I hope they are neither of them naturally bad; but, when we see such a vast difference between men dependent and men in power, any man who has any share of impartiality must fear for himself. My brother will tell you that I am proud, unindulgent, and hasty to take offence, but I doubt whether John Franklin will confirm it, although there is more truth in the charge than I wish there were. In this island, those malignant qualities are ostentatiously displayed and I am made to feel their sting most poignantly. My mind has here been taught a lesson in philosophy, and my judgement has gained an accession of experience that will not soon be forgotten.

In the days and weeks that followed, Matthew tried to gain an audience with De Caen on numerous occasions and wrote the first of many letters to him on 20th December:

Sir,

I would beg to ask you whether it becomes the French nation, even independent of all passport, to stop the progress of such a voyage of which the whole maritime world are to receive the benefit. How contrary is this with her conduct some years since towards Captain Cook. I sought protection and assistance in your port, and I have found a prison. Judge for me as a man, Sir — judge for me as a British officer employed in a neutral occupation — judge for me as a zealous philanthropist. What I must feel at being thus treated . . . With all respect due from my situation to the Captain General, I am

Your Excellency's obedient servant
Matt^w *Flinders*

Matthew's letter and requests went unanswered. He did learn, however, that an embargo had been placed on all foreign ships in the port, including two American ships which had been prevented from sailing.

After a time some of Matthew's books and charts were brought to him, with the notable exception of one logbook which De Caen retained for analysis. Matthew's only visitors were his jailer, the interpreter and a local surgeon who called almost daily

I sought protection and have found a prison

The all-powerful 'barbarian', General De Caen

to attend Matthew's ulcerated leg. He passed his days in writing letters to secure his release, including one to the Mayor of the town, and in working on a chart of the Gulf of Carpentaria. He also kept a detailed journal, in which he wrote:

> *Even my chart-making into which I have immersed myself as much as possible cannot prevent me from seriously reflecting upon the injustice, the haughtiness, and the Bastile-like mystery with which I am treated. I am kept from my voyage of discovery, from my country, from my family, and probably from promotion, and all this without being accused of a crime, and in direct opposition to the passport which had been obtained for me. This is indeed some return for the hospitality and assistance which the French ships* Geographe *and* Naturaliste *but now received at Port Jackson.*

In conversation with the interpreter, Matthew perceived that the reason for his detention was to give time for the voyage of the French explorer Captain Baudin to be published before his, but by mid-February he despaired in his journal:

> *Neither these three days or the preceding one did I see the interpreter or anyone else. I have received no answer or the least notice from the captain-general. I am yet a stranger to the cause of my confinement, and to the length of time it is to continue. It is indeed a most cruel suspense in which I am left. I know not whether death is not almost*

preferable to it, when accompanied with such contemptuous treatment as is bestowed upon me. Even in the dusk of the evening when I could see nothing, I am not allowed to stretch my legs with a walk, or to speak to any one except the interpreter, who has lately favoured me with very little of his company . . . It is useless to prove my innocence, for no crime is alleged against me. It is useless to write, for no answer or other notice is returned. It is useless to ask for an audience, for it is denied. What it will end in, God knows, the arm of oppression being once stretched out there is no knowing to what length it will go.

In April when a captured ship, a *'prize'*, was brought into port, it also brought the news that the story of the total loss of the *Porpoise* had been published in the Bombay papers. Unable to write to his family, Matthew knew that this would result in a great deal of unnecessary distress at home. He wrote in his journal:

this is a severe sting to us, since our friends will necessarily conclude us to be lost, and adds to my regret and indignation at being thus detained here against all the principles of justice and common humanity.

7

Adieu my best beloved — for a time

At one stage, so convinced was Ann of Matthew's death — he had not been able to write to her for two years — that she wore widow's mourning clothes. However, without the certainty of death there could be no funeral. There could be no gathering of friends and relatives to share the sorrow. There could be no healing process. There was only the indecision about what to do, what to say, and even whether to believe in his death.

There are many occasions on which Ann's friends attested warmly to her sweet nature, and described her as the most amiable of women. She was a person who was never known to be out of temper and she carried the strain of the separation deep within her. From a sunny disposition in her youth, this witty and generous woman grew to be racked with nervous ailments in middle age. They were the only outward expression of the turmoil, sadness and despair that — inside — inhabited her so wholly.

When at last the family heard from Matthew it was April 1804. The first of his letters to reach England were to Ann's stepfather. They alluded to Matthew's ill health, but a month later in another letter he wrote, '*I am in good health* [but] *I am wrung with anguish.*' The receipt of the letters was an indication of a relaxation of the conditions of Matthew's imprisonment. He and Mr Aken, his chief officer, had been moved to a prison which they shared with a number of other foreign captives. Officials from the town were allowed to call. Among the callers was a Charles Baudin, who visited Matthew on a strange mission concerning the propriety of taking a young woman from Port Jackson to India. Another caller was Thomas Pitot, who spoke some English but was very familiar with English books and English heroes. Pitot was to become Matthew's lifelong friend, advising him on the tone of his letters to the General and easing Matthew's access to the outside world.

A letter written in August was the first Ann was to receive but it made no reference at all to his health:

August 24, 1804
Redated with PS November 4, 1804

I yesterday enjoyed a delicious piece of misery in reading over thy dear letters, my beloved Ann. Shall I tell thee that I have never before done it since I have been shut up in this prison. The first day of January I dedicated to 'the pleasures of misery' and was violently tempted to go further, but I rushed into something else and escaped a further addition to the misery of recollection. It is a general and benumbing course of misery that I undergo in this imprisonment, but by dwelling on thy most charming letters every little of thy tender anxiety and distress, is afresh called up in vivid colouring to my maddened imagination. I am as it were shut up in a cask that has been rolled with violence from the top of hope down in the vale of misfortune; I am bruised and well nigh stunned out of my senses; but cannot thou imagine the addition it would be to this misery for the cask to have been drawn full of spike nails; — such is the increase of misery to my feelings on thinking intensely of thee.

I have many friends, who are kind and much interested for me, and I certainly love them, but yet before thee they disappear as stars before the rays of a morning sun. I cannot connect the idea of happiness with anything but thee. Without thee, the world would be a blank. I might indeed receive some gratification from distinction and the applause of society; but where could be the faithful friend who would enjoy and share this with me — into whose bosom my full heart could unburthen itself of excess of joy. Where would be that sweet intercourse of soul, that fine seasoning of happiness, without which a degree of insipidity attends all our enjoyments? From thee, my beloved, and thee only it is that I look to receive this zest for life, this height of luxury. Thou hast given me distressing

accounts of thy eyes and the state of thy health; I fear
to think it possible that attacks upon thee should have
returned since thy letter of Sept. 1802 was written from
Boston; but the cold weather is terrible for thee. O that
thou wast here in this genial climate. It is not at this time
too warm, and even in a prison we would be happy if
together. This is a large house in which eight English
officers now live. We have our own apartments and
servants, and a garden of about 2 acres in which we walk
[but] how earnestly have I desired to have thee with me, I
should hardly call myself unfortunate had I thy fond
delightful society. Couldst thou my dearest be satisfied to
be here? — I think indeed thou wouldst for a time; neither
wouldst thou be without female society. There were four
ladies taken prisoners, two have been permitted to go with
their husbands to India, and the others are living at a
house about 4 miles in the country . . .

I am not without friends even among the French. On the
contrary. I have several, and but one enemy, unfortunately
the last, is all-powerful here; or will he on any persuasion
permit me to pass the walls of the prison, although some
others who are thought less dangerous have had that
indulgence occasionally . . .

Did the governor know from what he keeps me, and
what extatic happiness awaits my return, the least spark
of humanity would be sufficient to make him hasten
instead of retard my departure, but the man has no
humanity for Englishmen . . .

It would indeed be delightful to meet thee there [in London] *and the moment I arrive I shall fly to Mr Bonner in Fleet Street for information. Heaven grant that no sickness, no misfortune may prevent thee from meeting me and being pressed to my enraptured heart. Indeed my Ann, thou knowest not how very dear thou art to me. At the same time that I respect and reverence thy very superior qualifications, I love thee most tenderly. I feel that thou art a part of me. Thy joys, thy pleasures, or pains are also mine. There is between us that sympathy which subsist between the different limbs of the one body; miserably torn asunder as we have indeed been but we will reunite, never more perhaps to be seperated, and our second marriage shall be more delightful than the first. Heaven grant that neither ambition, or necessity may ever again divide us . . .*

I think my dearest love, it would be useful to thy health to ride on horseback in the fine weather; thy strength suffers from want of exercise. Do not let a little expense prevent thee from any gratification of this sort. Buy a little horse, my love and take the air so often as thou canst, I am sure it will do thee good. We will so enjoy ourselves when I can get a few months in the country. We will make a tour amongst all thy friends and relations and mine, and for a little while no expense shall stand in our way.

Adieu, my best beloved, for a time. To thy good mother and Belle [Isabella, Ann's half-sister] *remember me most* kindly, — I am a letter in debt to the former but cannot pay it now. As for that idle thing, Belle, does she think I will bring her any pretty feathers or little fishes when she has not written one line for these live-long three years last past? No indeed, not a rusty nail! Now I dare say she would like a speckled piece of the coral reef upon which we were shipwrecked? Or a green octagon pebble from the top of the cloudy mountain? Or a stump shell brought up by the lead from 200 fathoms deep at the bottom of the sea? Or a little seahorse cased with horn as big as my thumb and taken out of the maw of a shark? Or perhaps a set of Trim's finger nails which he shed in the Gulph of Carpentaria? But not the least tiny bit will fall to her lot — I have some cockle shells that weigh a hundred pounds a piece, very convenient for wash-hand basins, and many other wonders too tedious to mention; I shall see about it when I come home; perhaps she may get one of them — no, I will give her a cage full of jumping spiders, as nimble as fleas, and about as big as small frogs. Won't they be a curiosity? Everyone has nine eyes and a little tail; and indeed they are thought by all who have seen them to be mighty curious.

Health, my dearest love, most anxiously do I wish thee. This is now a fine season in England. May thou be now happy in the enjoyment of it.

Thy most affectionate
Matt^w Flinders

What Matthew kept hidden from Ann was recorded in his journal on 29th September:

> *I am not positively ill, but not well enough to follow my pursuits with pleasure, arising in part probably from a depression of spirits. Pains in the legs, swellings in the glands of the neck, dimness of sight, and headache, are, however, sufficient to produce a depression of spirits, although the reflection of being a prisoner were not added to it.*

During his imprisonment Flinders wrote tirelessly to the Secretary of the Admiralty, to the admirals themselves, and to his captor's superior. Others, too, wrote on his behalf, to the French Minister of the Interior, to the Conseiller d'Etat, to Joseph Lalande the astronomer, and to Comte de Bougainville the navigator. In England, Sir Joseph Banks wrote to the President of the Royal Society and to the Institut National de France.

It was not until he thought, with false hope, that he was finally leaving Île de France that Flinders wrote on 4th November 1804:

> *At this time my health was very bad, and the sight of my right eye almost lost. The great use that I had for many years made of it, in taking astronomical observations, was probably the first cause of this misfortune; but its acceleration, and the derangement of my health, were owing to a want of active employment, and to the oppression of spirits which, in spite of myself, reflexions upon my situation too frequently occasioned.*

On 31st December he again wrote:

> *My health is much better than I could have expected, considering the nature of the climate and my imprisonment; and my appetite is so good that I believe it has an intention of revenging me on the governor by occasioning a famine in the island.*

It was a short-lived respite, for in January Matthew fell victim to a condition from which he had suffered ten years earlier, '*constitutional gravelly complaint*', which ultimately led to his death. (It was probably a complaint of the gall bladder.) In May he wrote again, making light of his problems:

> *For some time my health has been neither well nor ill, but such a mawkish kind of health as a prisoner, who was not much oppressed with any particular disease, may be supposed to have.*

It was during this period that Matthew wrote his twelve-page treatise on the influence of a ship's structure and fittings upon the readings of the magnetic compass. In it he was able to show how compass readings of fixed objects on the shore varied depending on the direction of the ship's bow — a subject he was to return to many times during his imprisonment. He employed himself in:

> *a demonstration of the quantity that ought to arise in the variation of the compass on changing the direction of the*

ship's head, supposing that change to arrive from a point of attraction in the middle of the ship, and the force of that attraction in comparison with that of the magnetic pole of the earth to be known.

Matthew's work on his beloved charts was halted temporarily with the loss of sight in his right eye, but he returned to them when he could in order to keep his mind active and his spirits distracted. When he believed his release was finally secured on 7th May 1805, he sent a number of his charts of Australia and a memoir ahead to the Admiralty. Several sealed packages taken from him on his arrival were returned, somewhat worse for wear, damaged by dampness and rats — all, that is, except the third volume of his logbook, which De Caen had put under close scrutiny to establish whether Flinders was a spy. It was never returned.

With the departure of his materials to England, Matthew's frustration at yet another delay to his own release proved understandably debilitating to his spirits and yet again to his health. His work continued as a distraction from his plight:

but what assisted most in dispelling this melancholy, was a packet of letters from England, bringing intelligence of my family and friends; and the satisfactory information that Mr Aken had safely reached London, with all the charts, journals, letters and instruments committed to this charge.

A number of Matthew's fellow prisoners had now been repatriated, leaving the island in American ships. Matthew and his long-time servant, John Elder, had been transferred to Maison Despaux, a house used as a prison, surrounded by 5½ acres of garden and high brick walls. The doctor allocated to the prisoners recommended that Matthew should be moved to the country to exercise and re-establish his health, but to little avail. By August, Matthew and John Elder were the sole occupants of the prison and able to walk in its gardens under the tolerant eye of the sergeant and his dogs. Matthew wrote of climbing the almond tree in the garden in the hope of sighting a ship in the port or at sea, but there were none to be seen.

In fact, Elder had been among the early seamen to be repatriated, but Matthew, in need of a servant, had asked that he remain in the colony. Elder therefore had a degree of freedom, and was able to run errands to the bazaar and to deliver Matthew's letters to the town officials and to De Caen.

While waiting for Elder to return from one of his errands, Matthew mused in his journal on Sunday 18th August:

> *Took three pinches of snuff, whilst I sat thinking of my wife and friends in England. Mm. Must not take so much snuff when I return, for it makes me spit about the rooms ... Took up my flute and played the 1ˢᵗ and 5ᵗʰ Duo of Pleyels Opera 9. Note, the first commences in a grand stile, and is sweetly plaintive in some parts of it ... Must have Pleyels musick when I return to England that is set for the flute, and Mozarts and Haydns and some of Hoffmusters and Duriennes, but the whole will be too expensive, musick is so very dear in England; and*

indeed so is almost everything else. Hope Mrs F will have got the better of the inflammation in her eyes, it is now fine weather in England and she will be able to ride out. Must take a house in the country when I return, and enjoy myself two or three months before I engage in any service, but, God knows, it is now three years since I heard from anybody at home, and what may have happened it is impossible to say . . . Would I go out as governor of a settlement . . . should it be proposed to me? I can't tell, it would depend on many circumstances. Wish to finish the examination of the whole coast of Australia before I do anything else. If there should be no great opening on the NW coast, it would be desirable to explore by land from the head of the great inlet on the south coast, and from Port Phillip . . . Half past three. Find myself a little sleepy. Don't know whether to go down and play a game at Billiards with the old sergeant, to drive it off, or to take a nap. Determined on the latter and laid down my bed.

In August Flinders wrote to his captor De Caen applying for permission to live at Wilhems Plains with his two servants at the plantation of Madame D'Arifat, '*an elderly widow lady, of an excellent understanding and disposition, and respectable character*'. It was a residence found for him by Thomas Pitot. The pressure generated by the many letters was effective at least to the extent that permission was finally granted, and at last on 23rd August Matthew was required to write and sign a condition of parole:

Adieu my best beloved — for a time

His Excellency, the captain-general De Caen, having given me permission to reside at Wilhems Plains, at the habitation of Madame Darifat, I do hereby promise, upon my honour, not to go further than the distance of two leagues from said habitation, without His Excellencys permission; and to conduct myself with that proper degree of reserve becoming an officer residing in a country with whom, his nation is at war: will also answer for the proper conduct of my two servants.

Matt^w Flinders

From then on, Matthew's captivity on Île de France was greatly improved, and his living conditions and lifestyle probably more luxurious than he would elsewhere have been used to. For his captor, De Caen, the pressure tactics had also had the desired effect, for it brought the matter to the attention of Napoleon, whom De Caen thought could then see for himself how well his general served him on Île de France, so vulnerably positioned for attack by the British fleet in the middle of the Indian Ocean. Napoleon decided that a generous gesture of release would not hurt his own plans and, on 21st March, De Caen's superior signed a document approving, but not ordering, Matthew's release. It took another four months for the signed document to reach Île de France.

Matthew revelled in his returned freedom, walking several miles before breakfast each day, exploring his new habitat and being welcomed by neighbours. He resided in a pavilion apart from the main house, with his two servants (Elder and Smith) in another. The discoverer and scientist in him were never at rest, so a walk into the countryside turned into an exercise to tax his mind. He wrote in his journal on 2nd September:

From the depth of water, and formation of the land round the lake Vanouce, I suspect it has formerly been the crater of a volcano; but at present I have not examined sufficiently about it to form a decisive opinion. I proposed with Mr Murat to visit the lake again in a few days, provided with fishing tackle and guns, and to explore round it in a canoe. I wish to ascertain whether the quantity of water which falls in, equals that which runs out of the lake, and from thence to know if there is any spring in it.

Matthew settled into his new life and into his new family: Madame D'Arifat, her two sons — Marc and Aristide — and three daughters — Sophie, Lise and Delphine. It is said Delphine fell in love with Matthew during his time in their residence. He enjoyed her company, flirted with her, and certainly spent many evenings with her. In his journal of 4th October he wrote:

I cannot say that, at present, I am very unhappy. Time has softened my disappointments, I have my books, am making acquisitions in knowledge, enjoy good health, and innocent amusements for which I have still a relish, and look forward to the hope of overcoming all objections and difficulties with honour to myself.

In the meantime, Ann continued to try to secure her husband's release, writing to the Admiralty inquiring as to whether they might present his case to the French Government.

Unaware of the progress already made, William Marsden of the Admiralty instructed:

> *Acquaint her with my compliments that no Cartel* [to exchange prisoners] *has yet been agreed upon, but that when it is, there can be no doubt of Captain Flinders being included.*

(Although 'cartel' today has the related meaning of 'an agreement between belligerent nations', the word was then used to mean ships which exchanged prisoners between nations.)

The colony was at war readiness and Matthew daily read the signal flag which told increasingly of *'cruizers'* off the port:

> [OCTOBER 1805] SATURDAY 12.—— *The red flag was down this morning, and the frigate therefore, as I suppose, out of sight: the pendant was up that bespeaks an embargo being laid upon ships in the port.*

> SUNDAY 13.—— *The embargo pendant was not up this morning. Today I accompanied our family on a visit to dinner at the house of a Mr Chevreau where we met the two young ladies from Madame Coves. It struck me what an acquisition it would be to our colony at Port Jackson, to have these five young, healthy, and agreeable young*

ladies transported there. They would not remain long unmarried; whilst in this island they will scarcely obtain husbands. Young women are much more abundant than young men here.

After our return in the evening, Madame was a little inquisitive concerning my voyages, the causes of my imprisonment here, my shipwreck, and finally of my family in England; in all which she seemed to take much interest. I satisfied the inquiries by producing such papers as best elucidated the heads of the different subjects, and giving the necessary additional information; but I added nothing more than answers to the questions. I did not say, that amongst my other grievances I had a beloved wife in England who was expecting my return in sickness and in tears; because I saw that the scene would become too interesting, and oblige me to retire. Madame and her amiable daughters said much to console me, and seemed to take it upon themselves to dissipate my chagrin, by engaging me in innocent amusements and agreeable conversation. I cannot enough be grateful to them for such kindness, to a stranger, to a foreigner, to an enemy of their country for such they have a right to consider me if they wish, though I am an enemy to no country in fact but as is opposed to the honour, interest and happiness of my own. My employments and inclinations lead to the extension of happiness and of science, and not to the destruction of mankind.

Thomas Pitot was a weekly visitor from town, riding three hours to visit his English friend. When business kept him away he found other means of communicating with Matthew, who wrote on 22nd October in his journal:

> *In the evening after dinner, my servant came to me with a letter from my friend Pitot, inclosing others from England, from my beloved wife, Sir Joseph Banks, Mr Robertson and some of my relations, from whom Mr R had been so good as to collect and forward them by an American brig, which arrived this morning from London: the latest letter is dated July 20 1805. From these letters I learn the very desirable intelligence of my family, and from Sir Joseph the prospect of an order being given for my liberation, by the interference of the National Institute. Immediately upon the receipt of these letters I hastened home to read them, for when I have any thing that touches me very closely, solitude is preferable to any company, especially of strangers.*

Madame D'Arifat had previously offered him accommodation in the house, but unsure how proximity to the family would suit him, Matthew had declined. Now, having made better acquaintance, he reconsidered his position:

> THURSDAY [OCTOBER] 24.— *Two days I had made a proposal to Madame D'Arifat to bring myself and forty piastres per month to her table, and this morning she gave me an*

answer in the affirmative . . . Accordingly I dined with her family today. She had before made me an offer to live with her without expense, which I declined; but I find the family so very agreeable and interesting, that I am become desirous of being so much with them as possible.

FRIDAY 25.—— *At present I rise every morning with the sun and go out to bathe in the river, which is tolerably cool work; afterwards I dress, and either accompany the ladies in a walk round the plantation to visit their poulaillers [hen houses], or read till half past seven, which is the usual breakfast time. After breakfast, I return to my pavilion to read and write for two or three hours; after which I take my dictionary and grammar, some paper and a book, and translate French into English, and English into French, and read French under the correction of Mesdamoiselles Delphine and Sophie, and they do the same in English to me: there late until or very near dinner time, which is at two o'clock. After dinner I read and write, or sometimes walk, and sometimes sleep until about 5 o'clock, when I join the ladies again, either in a walk, or in conversation before the house. After tea, which is usually served at half past six, we retire to the parlour for the evening, which is passed in reading French and English, in conversation, or sometimes in singing and flute playing, or sometimes at cards. At nine we sup, and at ten retire to bed, where the agreeable employments of the day often occupy so much of my thoughts as to prevent me from sleeping . . .*

THURSDAY 31.—— ... *I accompanied our family today to dinner at Mr Chazals where four or five different families were assembled. The evening was agreeably spent in dancing French dances, and waltzes; and gave me an opportunity of seeing them for the first time. Having been accustomed to our close modest English step, the high vaulting manner of dancing used by the French, did not appear so graceful or so decent as I should perhaps have otherwise thought it. In the dress of the ladies I remarked nearly the same singularity as I have before noticed in the account of them at the comedy. Very delightful, but not such as I should chose for females of my own family* ...

WEDNESDAY [NOVEMBER] 6.—— *The last two days have been employed in the usual manner. This family, particularly Mademoiselle D. become daily more interesting. She is indeed an extraordinary young lady, possessing a strength of mind, a resolution, and a degree of penetration which few men can boast of, and to these are joined activity, industry and a desire for information. 'Tis pity she had not been born a man, and in a more extensive field than the Isle of France* ...

MONDAY 11.—— *Mr Murat and I went to dine with Mr Chazal and the ladies by invitation, and I put my flute in my pocket in order to accompany Madame Chazal who is an excellent performer upon the harpsichord, and she has an excellent English instrument which had been taken in a prize, and for which she paid 1000 piastres. Our principal purpose was to conduct home the two young ladies, as yesterday, but it appeared that they dare not trust themselves with us for half a league; not, I believe, because they thought us mischievous, but for fear of the scandal of their society here. Thus the same ladies who dance with raked bosoms before a whole society, fear to walk half a league in open daylight with two gentlemen of their acquaintance. This is what I do not well understand.*

While Matthew enjoyed his new friends and new experiences, Ann remained bound to her saddened and lonely existence. The next letter which Matthew was to receive from England had taken more than three years to reach him. It was just as well that Ann's stoicism kept most of her distress from him, for much of her news was by now grossly out of date. Matthew replied:

Nov 20, 1805

Since Sept. 1802 I had known nothing of thee or any one of my relations and thy letter of that date had told me of the death of my dear father and of the miserable state of thy health. I knew not what to fear. I was obliged to drive as much as possible all reflection that related to England from my mind, to avoid being completely miserable; whereas now I can dwell upon the domestic scene my imagination continually raises with a solid and heartfelt satisfaction. I know that I have still a beloved wife whose

healthful frame is agitated only by her sighs at my absence:
she has no other distresses — delightful flattering thought.
And I now know also by this letter that steps have been
taken to obtain my release and that there is every prospect
of their being attended with success ... Receive my best
beloved, my thanks for thy communication, but especially for
thy sweet assurances of unaltered affection, and with them
receive my vows of constant unabated ~~fidelity~~* love: to love
thee more than I have done, and now do, I think cannot be,
thou has the sole undivided possession of my heart ...

The family [here] consists of three sons and three
daughters, four of whom are grown up and compose one of
the most amiable families this island can boast; but it is
with the eldest son, of about 27 years, and the eldest
daughter of about 20 that I have more particularly
attached myself. Thou canst not conceive how anxious they
are to see and be acquainted with thee. Tho unknown, I
scarcely think thou art less dear to Mademoiselle Delphine
D'Arifat than to many of thy relations. She talks of
making a voyage to England in the peace in order to see
more of our English manners and to make acquaintance
with thee ...

Comparatively with my situation in this island for the
first 20 months I am now very happy; and yet I often retire
to the little pavilion which is my study and bedroom, and
with my flute in my hand and sometimes tears in my eyes I
warble over the little evening song of which I sent thee a copy.

* Matthew's crossing out

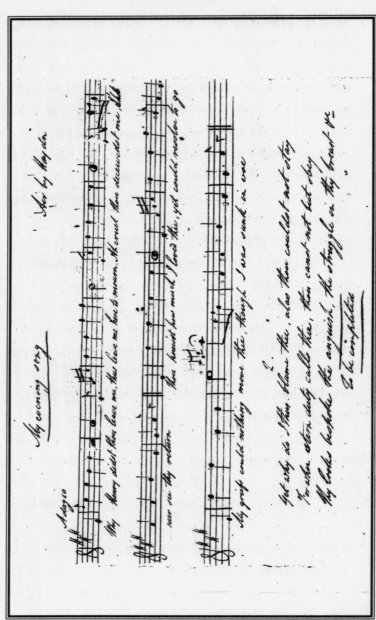

Haydn's Air: enclosed with Matthew's letter

Ah my beloved, tho my heart overleaps the distance of half a world and wholly embraces thee — From the letter I received from Sir J B, I expect that the first ship of war that shall arrive here from France will bring an order for my liberty . . . I am almost afraid, now to permit myself to expect with much anxiety . . .

In [Sir Joseph Banks'] *estimation, I treated them* [De Caen and his officers] *with too much haughtiness, and by that lengthened, or perhaps caused my imprisonment. I am sorry for this opinion which he seems to entertain, but it is very difficult for a man to treat another with respect, from whom he is conscious of having deserved well, but by whom he finds himself deprived of his liberty and otherwise ill-treated. Should the same circumstance happen to me again, I fear I should follow nearly the same steps . . .*

I think all my relations are becoming unfortunate in their concerns: they are all miserably poor. Notwithstanding my misfortunes I seem to be the luckiest of the whole.

Perhaps it was the sentiments of the Christmas season, or perhaps it was the effect Matthew saw he had upon Mademoiselle Delphine, but the entry in his journal that December records:

MONDAY 16 [DECEMBER, 1805].— *I formed the resolution of absenting myself more from home; in the afternoon therefore I paid a visit to Mr and Madame Chazal, and engaged myself to visit them again on Tuesday with my flute.*

On Boxing Day, Mademoiselle Delphine departed the plantation for an indefinite period to visit her brother in Flacq on the other side of the island. Whether she did so as a result of her growing affection for Flinders we can only guess. Matthew noted in his diary only that he had lost his best instructress for his French lessons. A letter he wrote to her at Flacq was more revealing:

My dear Miss D'Arifat,

Permit me on the opening of the new year to present you with my respectful compliments, and best wishes for your happiness during its continuance, and at the same time do me the favour of accepting a little fan, similar to two others your Mama has permitted me to present to your sisters: the smallness of its price is by no means a measure of my regard, but will demonstrate the sense I entertain of your delicacy and my fear lest you should refuse to accept a present that was of any value; for to have the little overflowings of friendship and esteem refused by those we admire and respect is a severe punishment to a heart possessed of any sensibility; you will not for a very trifle inflict it upon one you have ever honoured with the appellation of <u>friend</u>.

For your own sake I wish you all manner of happiness with your friends at Flacq, and every amusement the quarter can afford, but for my own interest I wish you may have a little solitary time in which to remember the absent. There is no fear that you might forget, for a moment, your excellent mother and your dear sisters and brothers, but there is a certain unfortunate Englishman at the Refuge scarcely as anxious of a place in your recollection as they, but who fears to be forgotten forever. His absence, at six in the morning, for example, you might sometimes think, 'Ah, they are now walking out at the Refuge to visit the fowls, I and my umbrella will be missed'. At ten, 'the school is now commencing, and they will be thinking of me. I wonder whether my sister is severe enough in her lectures with Mr Flinders. Has Madam A entered herself into the school or not? Does she make fewer errors in writing than I did. I should like to see the little circles upon her papers'. At dinner time, you might remember we are drinking to your good health, and may perhaps have a sentiment of curiosity to know whether Madam A drinks wine or not. In the evening, at whist you may still recollect us; and after supper, when you see the moon, it might remind you that I am taking a solitary walk beneath its beams; thinking sometimes of my beloved friends in England from whom I have been so long absent, and at the recollection of whom my heart melts within me; sometimes glowing with indignation at the unworthy and inhospitable treatment I have received from a nation who professes to patronise those very sciences whose service my life has been so often risked; at other times full of ardour at the prospect of very soon overcoming my difficulties, of convincing my enemies of their injustice, and receiving the honourable reward of my service; but still oftener than these, if you know my heart, you will remember, that in my evening *walks, I am thinking with admiration and gratitude of those individuals in this island, who in opposition to the vigour of their government have extended towards me the hand of consolation and even of friendship; and chiefly that good and kind family who have received me into their bosom, and of which, my friend, you are so bright an ornament. Excellent qualities of the head and of the heart which you possess, receive a double value in my estimation from the circumstance of their being combined in the person of one who distinguished me by the title of <u>friend</u>. Remember the expression in <u>jamais</u>, and if the word <u>doucement!</u> escapes your lips, remember the pain it once caused me. Your beauty — but this is the affair of your lover, and therefore no concern of mine.*

I very much hope that your time will be partly occupied in learning English with Madame Gonderville, both for your sake, my friend, as well as that you will then sometimes recollect your tutor. This caution you will say does not shew an over confidence in your friendship; but there is an old proverb which says 'women are fickle'. I cannot say that I have by any means found them so, but there is always <u>some</u> truth in old proverbs, and our acquaintance is but of three months standing yet. It would indeed be a miserable disappointment to find such a slanderous proverb verified in one who appears to possess a firmness of mind that few men can boast. It was my anxiety, rather than my fear, that made me commence this paragraph in the manner I did it in.

Adieu my best beloved — for a time

May I beg of you to present my compliments to your brother, and thank him for his remembrance of me.

From the excellent character I have heard of Madame Gonderville in your house, as well as from her being my countrywoman, I have the greatest desire to have the pleasure of her acquaintance. You will oblige me by presenting my respectful compliments to her, and if it should be my fortune to visit Flacq, before I quit this island, which is scarce probable, I shall certainly take the liberty of paying them in person. Adieu, my dear Miss D'Arifat, until we shall have the happiness to see your return to the Refuge, believe me to be with the highest respect and esteem, your affectionate friend, and most obedient humble servant,

Matt^w Flinders

There were undoubtedly temptations in Matthew's path, not only in the home of Madame D'Arifat, but all around him, now that he was free to go visiting. He wrote in his journal:

I was surprised to see so many handsomely dressed women in the [theatre] pit: ... their dress was beyond all comparison, more expensive and gay than those of the same class in England. The younger women were some of them very pretty, and there was one that might very well be called a beauty. Her age was said to be twelve years, but she seemed very womanish, though sufficiently modest, at least by comparison. The elder ladies seemed generally to be fat, but their dress was equally gay and bosoms equally bare with the younger. The necks of almost all, and the shoulders, and bosoms and nearly half of the breasts were uncovered, as well as the arms nearly up to the shoulders. They seemed to have good clear skins, and well turned necks and bosoms for the most part: and large eyes that were by no means destitute of power. An equal number of women, equally dressed would I think raise an uproar in one of our English theatres. The modest would be offended, the prudes would break their fans, the aged would cry Shame! The libertines would exult and clap, and the old lechers would apply to their opera glasses.

Not only fashion, but culture and religion in Île de France vexed Matthew's standards of acceptability. On 9th January he wrote in his journal:

In a conversation on religion, I found sentiments of tolerance pushed further even than mine. I believe, that Voltaire is pretty generally read amongst the married ladies here as well as in France; and that their fidelity to their husbands does not arise from religion, nor I think from fear of shame: little slips are spoken of, and laughed at, but do not prevent either one party or the other from being admitted into all societies.

In the meantime, history continued to be made elsewhere in the world. General De Caen's brother arrived from France with the news of the Emperor Bonaparte's sea battles with the English fleet and the death of Lord Nelson. From information gleaned in the port, Thomas Pitot told Matthew that there was little prospect of any change to his circumstances and endorsed Matthew's suggestion of writing to the General for deportation to France to stand judgement.

By now Matthew considered the reason for his continued captivity to be the same as had befallen the many travellers within France. The travellers had been detained as hostages for the return of ships and crews captured and held in English ports before the declaration of war. He felt cut off from almost every prospect of liberty before the termination of the war and at a loss for what other steps he could take to secure his freedom. He even considered asking permission for his servant, Elder, to go to England with letters for his family and to return with Ann. He went so far as to send a draft for £400 to the Reverend Tyler in case an opportunity for a suitable passage arose. However, the length and uncertainty of such a voyage caused him to waver over the question a number of times.

Matthew also contemplated escape, but on balance he considered this to be a last resort, only to be attempted after having his parole revoked, for he had given his word to act honourably. It was likely, too, that he would have had to flee without his precious charts and journals. It was a dilemma he confided to Mademoiselle Delphine and it was she who was able to persuade him of the foolhardiness of such a scheme.

Matthew visited the region of Tamarin with his friends in order to enliven his spirits, and succeeded in part.

He wrote:

> *I obtained a small portion of gaiety by it, but it does not*
> *penetrate very deep; indeed I fear the state of my mind*
> *is too much deranged for anything but a liberation from*
> *this imprisonment to produce a radical cure: my reason*
> *is become more and more weak and the imagination*
> *more and more strong, what may be the end I fear*
> *to think.*

In England, Ann continued to be not only emotionally destitute in the prolonged absence of her husband but also financially destitute. She had written to a friend in August 1806:

> *the Navy Board have thought proper to curtail my*
> *husband's pay, so it behoves me to be as careful as I can;*
> *and I mean to be very economical, being determined to do*
> *with as little as possible, that he may not deem me an*
> *extravagant wife.*

Her living expenses continued to be supplemented by her stepfather and she was able to live in his house with her mother and Isabella throughout the long years Matthew was absent. Matthew's exhortations for her to spend a little money on herself for the sake of her health show how removed he was from the reality of her meagre existence. He was the captive, but she was tragically deprived of the normal expectations of a life. She received a letter from him written many months earlier:

Adieu my best beloved — for a time

My best love. The hopes I had entertained of liberty, when I wrote the last, in Nov 20 1805, seem now almost dissipated. In continual expectation of arrivals from France, I delayed writing from week to week, and at last came an officer with dispatches; soon after arrived a frigate with other dispatches, and I waited in the utmost anxiety for some orders or intelligence from general De Caen. At length I learned, that my name was not mentioned in the letters he had received from the government — I wrote then to the general, again requesting him to send me to France, seeing that there was no probability of my situation being remembered by the French minister in the midst of the great interests with which they were occupied. His answer was, that he could not make any change in my situation before he should receive the orders of the marine minister; that by every occasion he had requested to receive their orders, and that he would again press him upon the subject . . .

At this moment, my hopes are indeed very feeble, I know not upon what point to fix them. Of themselves, it is most probable the French government will do nothing . . .

I have once thought of thy coming out here, should thou find that no orders have been given for my return to Europe, and should a good conveyance present itself. But the delicacy of thy health, the danger and inconvenience that might attend thee on the voyage, the difficulty of

finding a proper and confidential person to accompany
and protect thee, are too great to be overcome, buried, as
thou art in the country, and unacquainted with sea
affairs. Of all things in the world, I most desire thy
presence here, since I cannot come to thee; but of all
things in the world I should most dread thy undertaking
such a voyage without being protected and accomodated in
a manner which it is scarcely possible any opportunity
should place in thy reach. Let the conduct of a woman
on board a ship without her husband be ever so prudent
and circumspect, the tongue of slander will almost
certainly find occasion, or it will create one, to embitter
the future peace of her husband and family. Thou woldst
have first to go to America, most probably, and
afterwards embark on board another ship for the Isle of
France: but what a route for thee! I dare not think of it.
Only with all the concurring circumstances is it possible
— that thy health was good, that thou shouldst be
accompanied by a father, an uncle, or a brother, or that
thou wast acquainted with the captain of a ship, or some
respectable man coming here, who had his wife with him
and would undertake to protect and befriend thee . . . I
would then, my love, leave it to thee and to the judgement
of thy friends to decide . . .

I could not ask thee to undertake such a voyage, so much
do I dread the effects of the fatigue on thy health; and of
ten thousand circumstances that might occur to a person
whom I so entirely and so tenderly love . . .

Thee should indeed be very happy here, with this excellent family where I am placed; but what difficulties, fatigues, and risks thou wouldst have to arrive at this happiness. No, my dearest love it cannot be. I ask thee not to undertake it. As I said before, in the case of all circumstances above mentioned concurring to thy wish, I then leave thee and thy family and friends to decide; but if they do not all concur . . . my extreme concern and anxiety for thee oblige me to act the master, and denying my consent.

Matthew's life on the island swung from '*not being unhappy*' to periods of melancholy which persisted amid brief respites. He wrote on 28th October: '*Ate much, drank more, laughed a great* [deal], *forgot my unfortunate situation, and on returning* [home] *in the evening retired to my couch.*'

He remained generally in low spirits over a period of months, and in December 1806 he observed in his diary:

It is some time that I have not spoken of the state of my mind. I have so far overcome my propensity to melancholy reflexion, and no longer to experience that poignant anguish that so oppressed me in September and October last; but there is a weight of wanness at the bottom of my heart, that presses downward and enfeebles my mind. Everything with respect to myself is viewed on the darkest side. The little knowledge I have is not reckoned or is unappreciated; that of my actions which might bear the name of good, are depreciated. In society I have no confidence nor scarcely presence of mind; any little pleasantry either upon myself or the peculiarities of others, if they have any relation to, or seem to be thought to have any relation to me, puts me out of countenance. I am satisfied nowhere. When in company I wish the time came to break up, and when alone I am no more happy . . . I may truly say, that I have no pleasure in life: the nearest approximation to it is to forget my pain. How many little incidents are there in life, that we pass over rightly when in good health and spirits, but which afflict us under the contrary circumstances: that morbid sensibility to trifles is unhappily mine . . . Perhaps a restoration to liberty, and to my family might effect this, but I doubt if any less could do it.

Matthew's friends tried to distract him from his sorrows. Among them was his neighbour, Mr Chazal, who asked to paint a second portrait of Matthew, the first having been painted soon after his arrival at Wilhems Plains. It had shown the strain of ill health deeply etched in Matthew's face. The new portrait belied the sorrow within, painting a picture of handsomely suntanned good health and an aura of ease and confidence which is absent in other portraits painted of Matthew in England.

Matthew's servant, Elder, did not escape his own share of depression and melancholia, but in him it took a more serious shape. He became incapable of almost all work, grew suspicious, and saw treachery being plotted by everyone around him except Matthew. Even the family came under suspicion of plotting to do harm to him. At times it made Matthew angry, but it was an anger which turned to pity when he saw how miserable the man was, and how he tormented himself with empty shadows. So ill at ease did he become that Matthew took Elder to live and sleep with him in the pavilion, writing in his journal *'it is inconceivable the excesses of suspicion and distrust into which his imagination carries him. I tremble for the consequences.'* So intense did the melancholy and the suspicions of conspiracies become that servant and master agreed between them that a request should be made to the Captain-General for Elder's immediate repatriation to England. Elder himself delivered the request into the town. In the weeks of waiting for a reply, Matthew became convinced that his servant had become deranged. It was three months before the troubled man was allowed to board an American brig home via Baltimore. Preparations were made for his departure, and Matthew noted an immediate improvement in the condition of his servant's state of mind.

A replacement for Elder was readily available to Matthew. Slavery was still practised on the island and from time to time Matthew had employed one or more of *'the blacks'* to deliver messages for him to the town. The slaves were at liberty to work for themselves in their spare time, or to take leisure, and Matthew paid them half a dollar for their additional workload. During the maize-ripening season, when crops had to be guarded at night, he promised them an additional incentive payment if they returned early, for he wished to avoid any inconvenience to his neighbours.

For Matthew his liberty, too, seemed at last within reach. In July 1807, he received word from Sir Edward Pellew of a document sent to General De Caen imploring the General to set him at liberty. As well, a letter from the French Marine Minister, and approved by the Emperor, had also been forwarded to the General to secure Matthew's liberty and the return of the *Cumberland*. How the General intended to respond to these letters was not immediately known. Three days later, Thomas Pitot sent an express packet from the town containing a letter from Colonel Monistrol, the General's secretary:

> *I am charged to address to you the letter joined herewith, and to announce to you that as soon as circumstances will permit it you will fully enjoy the favour that has been granted to you by His Majesty the Emperor and King.*

What those *'favourable circumstances'* might be were left to Matthew's conjecture. Several days later the General's intentions were made clearer. Matthew had asked permission to travel to the town to arrange his affairs prior to departure. Monistrol made it clear that Matthew was no more at liberty than before the Emperor's favour had been granted. Circumstances were not yet appropriate for his departure and he was thus confined to the plantation.

Each time there was a neutral ship in port, or there was news of an exchange of prisoners between England and France, Matthew renewed his request for liberty. However, without a direct order to release him, De Caen continued to detain Matthew, refusing to return him to England to freedom, refusing to send him to France to face justice. For Matthew it was a heartbreaking time, liberty having been so unattainably near.

By late August Matthew received a letter from Monistrol inviting him, in the name of the Captain-General, to go to town to receive his remaining books and papers and other articles relating to his voyage of discovery. On doing so, Matthew inquired of Monistrol whether there was any determination over the manner and time for his departure. He was told unequivocally no. Not only were there no plans, but now there was even less hope than when the order had been written, for there was little or no communication between the governments of France and England. If demanded now, Monistrol warned, Matthew's liberation may well be refused outright.

With the continued delay in his release, and in low spirits, Matthew returned to Wilhems Plains, carrying with him a hint of the malaise which had so affected John Elder.

He wrote on 24th August 1807:

> *I was very much dejected on quitting the town, not immediately from the contrarieties I experience from the general, but from finding more and more as I examine into myself, how little I am fit for a public life or even holding a respectable place in society ... I am become more than ever timid, and afraid of ridicule; so that there is perhaps no personal danger that I would not encounter rather than the most trifling ... This was the true cause of my melancholy in September 1806 and I will be well if I am not thrown into a similar state again by my own reflexions.*

Nonetheless, rumours of his impending liberty persisted, to the extent that in September, when another prisoner-exchange ship anchored in the port, Matthew packed his books in readiness for departure at short notice. With his preparations complete, and time on his hands, he then set about making notes of the animals, plants, roots and trees on the island which he believed would be valuable for use in Australia.

The trying times had led to a quarrel with Mademoiselle Delphine some weeks earlier. He wrote in his diary on 19th July:

> *A little quarrel with my friend D which has now kept us at some distance for five or six weeks still continues to give me uneasiness. I was the party that had a right to be offended at what was said to me, but wished to pass it over; for which I am punished by opposition and neglect as if the case was the reverse.*

It continued for several months, with Matthew noting in his diary on 24th September:

> *The conduct of one of my friends in this house has continued to give me much pain these four or five months. My warmest friendship was first attracted by kindness and amiability of conduct almost unparalleled, which is now changed to its opposite, keeping just within the rules of decency for young ladies.*

Once again an exchange ship sailed without him. On 11th October Matthew wrote: '*It is inconceivable, the animosity of this barbarian* [De Caen] *to me. It seems as if he would never be weary of tormenting me.*'

By November, another exchange of prisoners was planned, and Pitot arrived at the plantation with the news that there seemed to be an intention of fitting a ship in which all of the English prisoners would be sent away. However, the General had also been heard to say that he had a prisoner here that he had great reason to be dissatisfied with, the prisoner's conduct having been very insolent from the beginning, and the government had in some measure left him at liberty to act as he should think proper regarding this man.

In January hope sprang again, and Matthew sent away three of his trunks to the town in readiness for whatever might happen, fearing bad weather would make the roads impassable just when he would be called to the port. Another exchange ship sailed without him. 1808 dragged on, and Matthew continued his daily routines of long walks, and exercising his mind with pure mathematics, with writings on accurately finding longitude and latitude, and of estimating distances at sea, and finally back to the '*Magnetism of the Earth*'.

It was a time which drew considerable sympathy for Matthew from Madame D'Arifat and her friends, who continued to rally around him. In August Matthew accompanied the family to Vacoas, '*Madame D'Arifat in a palanquin, Mr Labouve, myself, and Miss Delphine on horseback, and followed by about thirty blacks, carrying the luggage*'.

Enemy ships continued to taunt the port, cruising up and down in sight of land, like children teasing a dog with a stick. Occasionally the port was heard to bark back with gunfire from the bay when the ships came threateningly close to shore.

1808 portrait by Matthew's neighbour, Mr Chazal

1808 SEPTEMBER SUNDAY 4.—— . . . *This morning an English ship or ships was signalled to be between the Black River and Port NM. The cruizers from the Cape appear to have adopted the plan of being in with the land at daylight, so that it cannot be known from what quarter they come. This afternoon I began cutting a road in the woods towards a point from where I shall have a view of the sea to leeward . . .*

SATURDAY [OCTOBER] 22.—— *This morning Mr Cap-Martin sent me a letter from Mr Monistrol . . . in which he tells me from the general that 'having communicated to His Excellency the minister of marine the motives that had determined him to suspend my return to Europe, he could not authorise my departure until he received his answer upon this subject'. Thus all hope of my being sent to France on board the* Semillant *are at an end . . . I know very well that his true motives are personal animosity to me and a desire to prevent me from making known the injustice with which I have been treated . . .*

1808 DECEMBER SATURDAY 7.—— *. . . I read a letter of Mr Henri Frecynet; by which it appears that that part of the South coast of Australia discovered by me, as well as that first seen by Lt Grant and Mr Baudin is to be called Terra Napoleon; that Kanguroo island is to be called Isle Decres, and my two gulphs* [Spencer Gulf and St Vincent Gulf] *are to be named Golphe Bonaparte and Golphe*

Josephine. I know not whether to attribute the encroachment to ... the French government [for] there is very probably some connexion between them and my long detention in this island.

It appears Matthew's suspicions of the French Government were well founded. However, when the first volume of Captain Baudin's discoveries were published shortly afterwards in France, Baudin, if not the French Government, made honourable mention of Matthew Flinders' discoveries. A new atlas of historic and geographic charts was also published, with parts of the south coast of Australia, entitled Discoveries of Mr M Flinders and Baudin. Against their government, all the officers of the French exploration ships *Geographe* and *Naturaliste*, including Baudin, had applied to the Marine Minister for Matthew's liberation. Ironically, Matthew also received reports that it was generally thought in France and in England that he remained in Île de France because he chose not to depart.

By 1809 Matthew had again not heard from Ann for three years. Despair at his ever being released showed in his letters to her, in which he once more suggested she apply to the British Government for safe conduct to join him in Île de France, approval for which he had already sought from his captor. However, the times were hardly conducive to safe passage. Madame D'Arifat herself had cancelled a passage to Bourbon for the family at the last minute because of the number of warships cruising the seas around Île de France. The island was effectively blockaded, commerce suffered, government bills could not be honoured from France, and government officers' salaries were more than halved. The price of food, clothing and wine on the island had escalated alarmingly. Matthew found himself in the midst of friends who openly discussed the evils of the English with little regard to his presence.

Nevertheless, Thomas Pitot was able to continue to act as an agent for Matthew in cashing bills for him to live on, and Flinders' financial state of affairs on the island was such that he was able to purchase a small number of cattle. He wrote in his journal:

> *I purchased a full heifer from Mr Labouve, to be added to the cow and calf I had already; and I signed an agreement with him, by which he obligingly undertook to take care of these animals and their produce, for which I obliged him to accept of one-third of the produce. My intention is to leave thus the germ of a fortune which may in time become considerable, for even deducting the third, the capital should double itself in between three and four years.*

In August 1809 Matthew received a reply to his letter of 25th July informing him that the Captain-General would not oppose the residence of Ann in the colony. Matthew received the news with mixed blessings, for it also meant there was yet no end in sight to his imprisonment.

At last, on 13th March 1810 Matthew received a letter from the commissary of an exchange ship from England, the aptly named Mr Hope, who had received a promise from the government that Matthew could depart with him to India. Matthew was afraid to trust this news, having been similarly deceived before. Nonetheless, he wrote at once to his friend Pitot asking him to order some shirts, jackets and pantaloons for his shipboard journey. On 28th March Matthew received confirmation, by way of a letter from Colonel Monistrol, that the Captain-General had authorised his return to England in the prisoner-exchange ship:

> *His Excellency the captain-general charges me to have the honour of informing you, that he authorises you to return to your country in the cartel* Harriet *on condition of not serving in a hostile manner against France or its allies during the course of the present war.*

It was in Matthew's nature to cast out thoughts of what could not be. Now at last he let himself believe. He could not sleep, his mind and hopes released into activity. At one o'clock in the morning he was still awake, sitting by meagre flickering light to write his farewells to the many friends he had made and cherished on the island. The next day he took leave of '*his family*' and set off for the town. His departure from the island was again delayed, this time by the presence of warships cruising off the shore:

> *A schooner which came in sight was chased into the Bay du Tombeau by other cruizers, and a cannonading between them and the forts was heard until late at night.*

It was not until 8th May that Matthew was allowed to board the prisoner-exchange ship, but with further delays to their sailing, he and the other passengers again became virtual prisoners, their shore leave restricted. The same restrictions did not apply to residents of the island and, much to his surprise, a number of Matthew's friends rowed out in small boats to visit him and climb aboard the ship. May drifted into June and Matthew, still on board the *Harriet,* began learning the Malay language, *'this language may be useful to me in exploring the islands between Timor and New Guinea which I propose to do in my future voyage.'*

8

Out of the reach of General De Caen

On 7th June, a month after Matthew had first boarded the *Harriet*, an officer came on board to pay the prisoners their living allowances. Matthew wrote in his journal:

> *He brought also a parole for me to sign, promising me one [copy] of them before sailing, with a certificate from the Chief of the Staff of my being permitted to return to England.*

Two weeks later the ship was still at anchor, then at last:

> *. . . the pilot came on board at daylight, and the shore boats began to weigh the anchor, by which the ship is moored. Received some obliging farewell letters from my friends on shore, and visits from my good friend Thomy Pitot . . . Sent away my little black servant Toussint with*

a letter to Madame D'Arifat and a recompense, and took
Mr Herman, a seaman late of the Seaflower *as a servant.*
My sword was brought back to me, but could not hear of
my two spy-glasses.

It was nine in the evening before they made contact with the rest
of the fleet, and there it was quickly agreed Matthew could change
ship from the *Harriet,* which was set for India, to the *Otter,* which
was sailing for the Cape. On the day that the *Harriet* sailed,
Flinders wrote with joy and relief:

After a captivity of six years, five months and twenty-
seven days, I at length had the inexpressible pleasure of
being out of the reach of general De Caen.

At Capetown (which he had visited on an earlier journey, and
where he was known) Matthew was the centre of much interest
and spent his time being entertained and indulging in some
sightseeing while awaiting the arrival of a ship which could take
him on to England.

In September 1810, upon hearing from the Secretary of the
Admiralty, Sir Joseph Banks wrote to inform Ann of the long
awaited news. She had already been forewarned by John Elder in a
letter to her, on his return to England, that the Captain '*does not*
look so well as he did by a great deal, his red . . . cheeks is certainly gone, and
his hair is very white.'

Flinders arrived back on 24th October, nine years and three
months after he had left. With the ship at Spithead, Matthew went

ashore, arriving in London at seven o'clock on 25th October to find news that Ann was in town. He hastily arranged lodgings and called upon the Admiralty before at long last meeting with Ann at noon.

Ann and Matthew's reunion was witnessed by John Franklin, his cousin and former crew member. Franklin wrote to Matthew afterwards, explaining the abrupt manner in which he departed Flinders' welcome home:

> *I felt so sensibly the affecting scene of your meeting Mrs Flinders that I would not have remained any longer in the room under any consideration; nor could I be persuaded to call a second time that day.*

Ann had spent less than three months with her husband immediately after their marriage. And now in appearance, health, and experiences he was a greatly changed person. In spite of their long and loving letters, their physical proximity had to be re-learned. There were matters of more permanent lodgings to be found, family to be reunited with, friends to see, and all these juggled with the wish of Ann and Matthew to spend quiet days together.

Their time to themselves was brief, for Matthew was obliged to meet with the First Lord of the Admiralty, Mr Yorke (after whom Flinders named Yorke's Peninsula), and to visit the Transport Office to inform them of the state of the *Cumberland*. He also had to attend to such matters as getting his hair cut, and being measured for a suit of clothes for the colder English climate.

Mr Yorke offered him a promotion dating from the time, just a few months earlier, when he had embarked in the prisoner-exchange ship. Matthew was quick to present his case for it being dated considerably earlier, to which Mr Yorke seemed well disposed. However, the following day Matthew received a letter from the Admiralty announcing his promotion to post captain from 7th May, the commencement date of Mr Yorke's authority in the Admiralty, for the First Lord believed he could not and should not date any promotions prior to his own term of office. Matthew considered this entirely unjust in view of the work he had continued to carry out while imprisoned, and regarded it as a further extension of the punishment handed out by De Caen. As long ago as 1807, however, Matthew had foreshadowed their response, when he wrote to Ann:

Many promotions have taken place since my absence, but I have no hope of being included in any before my return, and I fear, that those with me will remain in the same predicament. If, however, I should succeed in making the government sensible to how unjustly I have been treated, I may perhaps obtain my promotion from the date of my imprisonment.

His patron, Banks, sympathised with Matthew but only His Majesty King George III could amend the date. Unfortunately King George, whose mental health was worse than Matthew's physical and financial plight, was in no position to apply himself to matters of state. The Prince Regent agreed with the First Lord. There was little further that Matthew could do, and he accepted the four shillings per day, the half-pay of a post captain ashore.

Ann and Matthew took up residence at 16 King St, Soho, while Matthew sorted out his affairs, including a small inheritance from his father's will. He set about claiming back-payment of allowances from the Admiralty, and payment for work undertaken for the East India Company.

In contradiction to their formal stance, Flinders was fêted with '*flattering attention*' by the Admiralty. Banks gave a dinner in his honour at the Royal Society, and Bligh took him to meet the Duke of Clarence (later King William IV), who had expressed a wish to meet him and see his charts first-hand.

For Ann, Matthew's voyages were not yet truly over. Matthew had brought with him letters and money for the French prisoners held in England and, after visiting them, worked actively for their release and repatriation. He relived his voyages constantly, since his main employment was the writing of *A Voyage to Terra Australis*, for it was '*their Lordships intention to cause it to be published in the form of a narrative, drawn up by the Commander, on a plan similar to that pursued in the publication of captain Cooks voyages*'.

It was not until 23rd November that husband and wife left London for a six-week holiday in Lincolnshire. They rose early, breakfasted, and set off for the White Horse Inn to catch the Cambridge coach, missing it by five minutes and being forced to hire a hackney coach to catch up with their fellow travellers for their 51 mile journey. They travelled all the following day by post-chaise to rendezvous with friends and assorted family members. The visit was marred by Ann suffering a severe headache, reminiscent of the pains that had tormented her father. On her recovery, the pair journeyed on to Hull to stay with Matthew's favourite cousin, Henrietta, and her husband. Matthew wrote happily in his journal:

Wind Northerly and weather mild for this time of year. I went with Mrs Flinders about Partney to visit her old friends, nurses, servants and to all of whom she wished to show her lion, and to give some trifle.

In Hull they also saw '*the steam engine, made by Watt, by which the water that supplies the town, is raised to the level necessary for that purpose: Mr Atkinson, the superintendent, was very obliging in shewing and explaining.*'

The day after New Year they caught the noon coach from Barton, dined at Lincoln, supped at Falkingham, breakfasted at Stilton, dined at Baldock, and reached their lodgings at ten the following night after an absence of six weeks, having been thirty-four hours in the coach.

Two days later Ann was again confined to bed with a severe headache which seemed to recur every two to three weeks.

Matthew met again with Mr Yorke of the Admiralty, who referred the publication of the voyage of discovery in the *Investigator* to a committee made up of Sir Joseph Banks, a Mr Barrow and Matthew. It was agreed that the Admiralty would pay the expense of reducing and engraving the charts, landscapes, figures, and the natural history illustrations. Sir Joseph was authorised to superintend all the work and to make arrangements for all expenses.

The writing and printing of the volumes was to be at Flinders' own cost. He or his heirs then retained the right to all copies printed, with both the profits and losses in the exercise being at Flinders' risk.

From then on, all Matthew's other engagements and thoughts of any future voyages were subservient to the completion of his volumes. The need to be close to paper suppliers, engravers and printers as well as to the committee, for consultation, would keep Matthew in London instead of residing in the countryside, and he asked if the Admiralty would put him on full pay to make up the difference in living expenses which this would entail. This, however, was deemed to be out of the question for fear of setting a precedent, and Matthew calculated that the publication would therefore cost him £500 or £600 (notwithstanding the fact that he could not take on any paid employment).

The result of these discussions led to Ann and Matthew moving quickly to other lodgings at No. 7 Nassau St in Soho.

The Hydrographer's Office returned Matthew's charts and journals, and life settled into a routine, with Matthew working on the volumes from seven in the morning until sunset. The day was broken only with business calls in the town and, when the weather was fine, a half hour to an hour's walk with Ann after the midday dinner. They walked into the city, sometimes to the park, and on other occasions visited London's art galleries and museums. Once, on being caught in a thunderstorm, Matthew wrote, *'walked out with the ladies, a thunderstorm came on before we could get home again, and wetted and frightened them very much.'* After tea they occasionally played chess and Matthew taught his brother and Ann to play tric-trac, which had been such a popular pastime on the Île de France. On Sundays Ann went to church, often leaving Matthew to work on his journal. At other times he accompanied her, and then would visit Sir Joseph Banks for his regular Sunday evening *'conversation'* gatherings. They dined often with friends or with Samuel Flinders, who was a regular visitor and keen to help his elder brother in calculations arising from the eclipse Matthew had observed on 4th March in 1802.

On 13th February they learnt that the guns in England had been fired to announce the taking of the Île de France, upon which the Admiralty asked Matthew to write up his observations on the island to assist in the planning for their new territory. The following month a packet of letters from the island was received with news of the D'Arifats and friend Pitot. The packet also enclosed a letter from Ann to Matthew, now three years old.

Samuel's frequent visits to the Flinders household did not always pass peacefully and on one occasion, after visiting friends, Matthew wrote that he had noticed a disagreeable trait in his brother's character, which hurt him. Samuel was anxious to pursue his promotion in the navy and enlisted his brother's help, whereupon, to Matthew's shock, the Admiralty informed him that the younger Flinders' promotion had been stopped as a result of his court-martial on board the *Bloodhound* for disobeying orders.

In February, Matthew suffered another one of his infrequent *'gravelly'* attacks during the night, with fever and shivering. Nevertheless, it was Ann who appeared to be the more sickly of the two, and in May the doctor was called four days in a row to attend upon her. On the fourth day, Matthew wrote, *'Dr Dale called and prescribed for Mrs F, after which I accompanied him home to dinner, where was a large party.*' The following day Ann seemed to have recovered remarkably and walked out with Matthew and her sister Isabella to view the illuminations for the King's birthday.

Ann's bilious headaches were debilitating, and Matthew wrote despairingly how they destroyed almost every pleasure in her life, so frequently did they occur. Fortunately, the day after each attack she was usually sufficiently recovered to walk out with her husband.

On 1st July Ann suffered what was to be the last of her bilious headaches for another nine months or so. Pregnancy was not a topic for discussion in the nineteenth century, and even in Matthew's private diary he makes no mention of Ann's condition other than that their evening walks increased in frequency, and obliquely, when she was four months pregnant, that she suffered a severe haemorrhage:

> *Mrs F taken very ill this morning with a suppression, which became so bad, that Mr Adams the apothecary found it necessary to apply a catheter. This prevented me from doing much at my chart.*

At Ann's age the pregnancy must have caused some concern, both for the health of the mother-to-be and for the infant.

In the meantime, they again moved lodgings — at the end of August they shifted to Mary Street–New Road, which at £45 was £19 less per year than their previous residence.

The move taxed Ann's strength considerably, but they were pleased to be close to fields where they could walk in the afternoons while still being within reach of London. John Elder

visited them there, and Ann and Matthew were pleased to find him
well recovered from his mental sufferings on Île de France.

In November Matthew again found himself laid low with '*a fit
of the gravelly*', but like Ann's headaches, they seemed to be
debilitating for usually no more than twenty-four hours.

Matthew continued industriously on the production of his
volumes and found he had friends in high places to help him. He
had cordial relationships with Sir Joseph Banks and Admiral Bligh.
He wrote:

> *Met Admiral Bligh, and had a long conversation upon his
> passage through Torres' Strait. On returning home, sent
> him the extract from my introduction relating to that
> passage, to be submitted to his approbation or correction.
> My brother dined with us upon a goose sent from
> Donington . . . Rec'd a note from Sir JB and went to him
> and Admiral Bligh; when names were applied to the
> islands discovered by the latter in Torres' Strait . . . Rec'd
> a letter from Admiral Wm Bligh, proposing to accompany
> me to His R H the Duke of Clarence, who had expressed
> a desire to seeing general chart of Terra Australis.*

Samuel's activities continued to worry his elder brother for, in a fit
of pique at the navy, Samuel had decided to retain the books of
Matthew's voyage which he had been using for his calculations:

> *My brother came to dine. On his going away I requested
> him to deliver me all the books not belonging to himself;*

when I found to my surprise, that he laid a claim to such of my books as had either wholly or in part, been written in by himself ... which I consider to be highly condemnable in many points of view; they having been confided to him to be used for the benefit of my voyage. This strange conduct in a brother, affected me much ... Mr Crossley came by appointment and after examining how far the calculation could be carried on without the books we went to Sir Jos. Banks. I found that, in all probability, a prosecution against my brother would be entered by the Board of Longitude for the books, and that the end of it [for Samuel] would be not only the loss of all future advancement in the Navy, but probably the being scratched off the list of lieutenants.

Samuel agreed to return the books to Matthew as a personal favour, and the unpleasant matter was put to an end.

At the end of the year, Ann and Matthew's expenses exceeded their income by £197, a factor of their having to live in London. As a consequence, they moved lodgings once more, this time to Mary Street–Brooke Street, where a respectable family was able to accommodate them, but in less pleasant surrounds, for £15 less per year.

In March, Isabella Tyler came to stay with them for an indefinite period to assist Ann through the final stages of pregnancy. On 1st April 1812 Matthew wrote in his journal, '*this afternoon Mrs Flinders was happily delivered of a daughter to her great joy and mine.*' This was the first mention of Ann's pregnancy in his personal diary. At the time of daughter Anne's birth, Ann was 42 years of age, and Matthew 38 and in failing health — he had another attack of the '*gravel*' just days after the birth of their daughter. Ann, however, recovered remarkably well from her confinement, with Isabella attending her and with her close friend, Mrs King, visiting the new family.

The sensibilities of the time did not encourage Matthew to write deeply of such intimate matters, and it is ironic that the only known letter from Ann to Matthew which has survived over a century conveys the very private dread and fears which a mother-to-be faced in that time, particularly an older mother-to-be. The letter, written before the birth of their daughter, was to be read by him should she have died in childbirth.

Even in the midst of her own fears, Ann's first concern was for Matthew's future happiness:

My dearest Love

As life is at all times uncertain, & as there is a friend approaching, which may Alas! terminate mine, I mean that Hour of Nature's sorrow, which may either make us the delighted Parents of a dear Infant, or consign me to the cold tomb, reducing thee to distress and loneliness, & that Infant shoᵈ it live, to a Motherless Babe — The thought is infinitely painful, yet I feel a wish to leave a few lines for thy perusal, when I am no more, shoᵈ it be the will of Heaven to take me thus soon from thee — Oh my Love! I pray that the Almighty may in mercy spare me in the *awful conflict which awaits me, the idea of a separation is dreadful, & more especially a separation by Death, it will be hard indeed to give thee up, so soon, after so long an absence — but perhaps it must be, Oh if such is the will of Providence, may Heaven grant me composure and resignation in the painful moment, may it enable me to resign my blessings, & thou the first & best of them, into the hands of that bountiful Creator, who bestowed them on me, without a murmur — sho^d I indeed be taken from thee, Oh remember me my precious Love, but I know thou wilt at times, even sho^d another take my place — which I view as a <u>certain</u> circumstance, nor can I wish the contrary, because I would have thee happy, which I know thou couldst not be, without a companion, formed as thou art to enjoy domestic felicity with so high a relish — I trust thou wilt meet with some amiable character, who will love thee with fervour & unfading affection as <u>I have ever</u> done. May it be her chief study to make thee happy — & Oh my Love, sho^d Heaven spare the life of my Babe, teach her to be kind to it, and sho^d she give others to thy ease, Oh let not <u>mine</u> be neglected, but let it ever share in thy fond affection, Oh my Love remember this is the petition of Her who loved thee with unabated tenderness for years — but I know thou wilt be kind to the previous Charge I may leave thee, for is it not thine own as well as mine?*

Let thy portrait be kept for the child, sho^d it live — sho^d it not, dispose of it as thou pleasest — remembering how dear it was to me in those hours, those <u>years</u> of misery &

absence — Could the lifeless Image speak, it might tell
with what heartfelt anguish it hath often times been
pressed to my lips, been bedewed with my tears — but
enough, I know so long as Memory remains perfect & thy
reason maintains its throne I cannot be forgotten — I
shall leave a written paper with a few arrangements of
what I could wish to be given to those friends whom I have
valued most thro' life, & which I know thou wilt indulge
me in the disposal of — sho^d my sister be here at the time,
she will I hope undertake the task of sending the few
trifles I speak of, according to my wishes — My wedding
ring is thine, & I should like thee to wear it for my sake,
on thy little finger, if it will fit there — remember it was
the pledge of union, of faith, of love & of all which
renders domestic life happy.

I have yet another request — which is that thou wilt
read the holy scriptures, & that thou wouldst try to <u>pray</u>,
I know & feel fully confident that God both hears and
answers pray — Oh my precious, <u>precious</u> Love, pray
earnestly that we may meet in Heaven — Thou mayst
gain reputation, fame, fortune, honour in this life, but Oh
sweetheart these fading vanities have no tendency to qualify
the soul for the kingdom of God — Accept my best Love,
my most heartfelt acknowledgments for all thy kind
attention to me both in the hours of health & sickness —
thy kindness hath often soothed me when in pain, &
caused me to bear it with more patience, more resignation
— Again, accept my grateful thanks — I owe thee still,

(much & ardently, as I have loved thee) a World of affection & tenderness, Oh may a gracious God be pleased to spare my life, & enable me to shew it thee for several years to come, perhaps he <u>will</u> be merciful, & aiding me with strength bear me thro the approaching conflict — Grant it heavenly Father, if it be thy blessed will, but Oh prepare me thro the merits of thy dear Son, for whatever dispensation thou art pleased to appoint for me — I feel I cannot yet say farewell — I shall perhaps address thee again, ere the dreadful hour of conflict arrives — The writing this hath cost me many tears —

AF —

Happily, Ann's fears did not materialise.

She was in fortunate good health and Matthew was able to travel to Sheerness then Portsmouth in May, at the request of the Admiralty, to take compass bearings from the ships lying at anchor there. His purpose was to accurately calculate the influence which iron structures on the ships might have on those readings. He wrote from Portsmouth in his journal on 19th May:

I took the dips of the needle whilst the ship's head was East, and found it to be less than on shore, which I attribute to the attraction of the guns on each side of the ship . . . but on the fore-castle the dip was greater, owning perhaps to the coppers, as they are called and a greater quantity of other iron under the fore-castle than elsewhere.

The results of Matthew's investigations were published by the Admiralty and ultimately led to a correction factor in compasses, still known today as the '*Flinders Bar*' (it was to become increasingly important over the years, as ships were built with much more iron work). While he was away he wrote almost daily to Ann, and when he returned home found '*my poor little child*' unwell. A few days later a wet nurse, who lived close by, was called in to take the child with her, for Ann was unable to feed her newborn sufficiently.

Earlier that month, on 7th May, Ann, Matthew, Isabella and the wet nurse had taken the child to the church of St Giles in the Fields, where she was christened by the name of Anne. The wet nurse then took little Anne home and the others continued on to Bullock's Museum to see a fine collection of natural history '*tastefully displayed*'.

The birth of his daughter had prompted Matthew to attend to his will and, optimistic of the sales his volumes on Terra Australis would generate, he generously left legacies to his extended family, an annuity to his stepmother, the erection of memorial tablets to the three previous generations of Flinders and the gift of eight mourning rings to friends.

The parlous state of their finances led to the family moving house six times. In spite of the hardships and the turbulence of their existence during these years, Ann was to write of her husband, in a letter to a close friend:

> *I'm well persuaded that very few men know how to value*
> *the regard and tender attentions of a wife who loves them.*
> *Men in general cannot appreciate properly the delicate*

affection of a woman, and therefore they do not know how to return it. To make the married life as happy as this world will allow it to be, there are a thousand little shades of comfort to be attended to. Many things must be overlooked, for we are all such imperfect beings, and to bear and forbear is essential to domestic peace. You will say that I find it easy to talk on this subject, and that precept is harder than practice. I allow it, my dear friend, in the attention for uniform tenderness and regard. I have nothing unpleasant to call forth my forbearance. Day after day, month after month passes, and I neither experience an angry look nor a dissatisfied word. Our domestic life is an unvaried line of peace and comfort. And o, may heaven continue it such, so long as it shall permit us to dwell together on this earth.

Matthew worked incessantly upon *Terra Australis* and was under pressure from Banks and others to complete the documents. He was critical to the extreme in the reproduction of his charts, making 92 corrections on one page alone, with directions to strengthen the coastline, make the dot distinct, and so on.

Ann was able to assist her husband, checking his transcriptions from their original manuscript with him. Diversions became increasingly less welcome to Matthew but he found time to travel with Ann to the Strand to get his silhouette taken and also to collect it four days later. One of the few interruptions which Matthew did allow himself was to conduct business in London on behalf of his old friend Thomas Pitot, for whom he exchanged bills at the Treasury and converted ingots. He also continued to work for the release of the prisoners from Île de France and in 1813 finally received the news that all were to be freed.

Once again Matthew's diary records that Ann went for several months without a violent headache, although Matthew reports her as feeling '*unwell*' from time to time. There was no mention of a pregnancy until in January 1813, when he wrote that she had miscarried, and several days later, '*Mrs F not yet recovered from her accident*'.

In February they went looking for new lodgings, '*being unhappy with the conduct of their landlady and some of her lodgers*'. On this occasion the move was to 45 Upper John Street, where they took all of the first and second floors plus a kitchen for £95 per year, slightly more than Mary Street, but the lodgings were newly furnished and the owners appeared to be respectable.

The move was again short-lived — Ann and Matthew once more found themselves packing trunks, this time moving to No. 7 Upper Fitzroy Street at an additional £5 per year. In July, after an absence of fifteen months '*our little Anne was taken home today, from nurse, where she had been . . . She now runs stoutly, and though able to say very few words makes herself understood.*' Whether she was returned home for medical reasons, or whether a problem was quickly perceived by her parents, a week later the child was operated upon '*in whom a part was discovered to be closed which ought not*'. Teething was also soon upon the new parents, something which little Anne did not take to easily.

By October, Matthew was well into the proofing stage of his volumes:

FRIDAY 1.—— *Occupied examining proof sheets, working at the chart of Torres Strait, and copying and comparing astronomical observations.*

OCT SAT 2.—— *Called on Mr Arrowsmith to speak to the engravers of the charts. Found that, to have them done satisfactorily I must attend them rather closely. Went on to Fleet Street on business. Afterwards compared the narrative with the chart of Torres' Strait, which was finished yesterday as far as my sheet on the large scale takes it in. In the evening, occupied with the astron. Observations, and examining a proof sheet.*

9

The beginning of the end

In February 1814, the Flinders again moved house, this time to 14 London Street, close to the Transport Office. The day before their move, however, Mr Hayes the surgeon was called to Matthew to attend to his *'gravelly complaint'*, which was said to be either a stone or gravel in the bladder and which had been troubling him for some months, becoming increasingly painful. The doctor now called every two days to attend to Matthew. It was the beginning of the end.

Matthew was in considerable pain and could attend to his proof sheets for only short periods at a time. The surgeon passed a bougie, a slender flexible instrument into the bladder, but found nothing much of consequence. Samuel ran errands for his brother to the bank and to the engraver, while Matthew became increasingly afraid to move about. When he did walk, he was forced to move in what he described as a *'snail-like'* manner.

He was prescribed calcined magnesia for some time until the crystals which he passed were analysed and were thought to have been exacerbated by the magnesia. He was then given distilled water. (Calcined magnesia is still used today as a treatment for gastric ulcers, but what is now known is that magnesium oxide has low solubility and, in heavy and continuing doses, will crystallise through the kidneys if sufficient water is not taken to help dissolve the residue.) Matthew took citric juice, and tea (which relieved him more than the medicines). Then he was prescribed muriatic (hydrochloric) acid, gum arabic in barley water, and finally castor oil and seltzer water. He became daily worse, his need to '*make water*' increasing from eleven, to twenty, to thirty-six, then fifty-two times in twenty-four hours. This alone kept him exhausted from lack of sleep, his flesh and strength wasting away. Sitting down was painful for him and a hollowed cushion was fashioned to allow him to sit for half an hour at a time, after which he was obliged to lie down on the sofa.

In his diary on 26th March, Matthew described his ordeal in all its awful detail:

> *Continue to pass gravel, consisting of oblong small crystals, some bright, others discoloured with blood . . . these crystals have always been more or less enveloped in mucus forming a pulpy mass . . . the detached pieces feeling to be too large for the passage. Had more pain today, and the urine more red than lately.*

On 1st April, the outlook was no more positive:

> *It appears that the crystals have been produced by the magnesia, and were not, as I had hoped, pieces detached*

from the stone in the bladder. It is rather to be feared that some of them may have been added to it. It is certain that the irritation at the neck of the bladder has increased lately, and that generally I am worse.

Although he was still only thirty-nine years of age, Ann wrote to a friend that Matthew was worn to a skeleton and had aged so rapidly that he looked like a man of seventy. By June the surgeon provided him with opium pills to reduce the pain of an abscess caused by the passing of the crystals. Isabella arrived to help Ann nurse him, and in the midst of all this little Anne came down with measles, a common but severe childhood illness in those times.

On Sunday 26th June a copy of Matthew's account of the voyage and the corresponding atlas was delivered to Sir Joseph Banks by the printers, in time for his Sunday evening gathering. Three days later Mr Arrowsmith brought Matthew a set of proofs of all the charts of the atlas. Matthew expressed his delight with the engravings and wrote a note to that effect to Banks.

On Sunday 10th July 1814, Matthew wrote '*did not rise before two, being I think, weaker than before . . .*'. They were the last words recorded in his diary.

10

What I now
and must ever feel

The leather-bound copy of the completed book arrived from the publishers, G and W Nicol of Pall Mall, as Matthew was dying. Ann laid the volumes in his bony grasp. He did not regain consciousness, but she believed he knew his life's work to be complete. Perhaps the words she was to write in her memoir of him dwelt somewhere in her mind:

> *Indeed, so strong was his inclination for this dangerous service that amongst his friends, he has been frequently heard to declare his belief that if the plan of a Discovery Expedition were to be read over his grave, he would rise up awakened from the dead.*

On the morning of 19th July Isabella was woken by the sound of Ann crying:

*She was going to the sick room — I begged her to let me
go first — The sun shone brightly on me as I went down
the stairs, all seemed still . . . I entered the drawing room
— his bedroom opened into it, the door was open — I
went in — there lay the corpse, the spirit flown, his
countenance placid & at rest — Dear Matthew! — I
stood at the foot of the bed contemplating the scene for a
few moments, then rushed up stairs to my Sister — She
was soon in the room of death & pressed his cold lips to
hers — it was a heartbreaking effort . . .*

*Her dear babe . . . the poor child felt that something very
dreadful had happened, but did not know what — &
putting her little fingers to wipe the tears from her Mother's
eyes, she said, 'Don't cry Mamma'.*

Matthew Flinders died aged forty years four months and three
days. He was buried in the graveyard of St James Chapel in
Hampstead Road. His daughter, on visiting the grave many years
later, found the site greatly altered, the tombstones removed, as
had been the graves and their contents — his whereabouts
forevermore unknown.

After Matthew's death, Ann wrote to his closest friend,
Thomas Pitot, who had befriended him on Île de France, today
known as Mauritius. He was someone with whom she continued
to correspond, and who continued to act as an adviser to her in
matters of business for many years.

My dear Sir

How much will your affectionate heart be grieved, when you shall be acquainted with the mournful intelligence of the death of my <u>dear husband</u>, which took place on the 19th of July last, after a painful & <u>most distressing</u> illness of five months. I need not attempt to describe to you, who in some measure knew his worth, what my emotions were in being deprived of such a husband, such an invaluable friend, nor what I <u>now</u> & must ever feel from such a loss — in fact did I feel the deprivation a thousand times <u>less</u> than I do, language is <u>so</u> poor, that I could only speak of it in the same words. A character so <u>exalted</u> in <u>every</u> point of view, as his was, I never expect to behold again, & I trust I shall be pardoned when I say, that in comparison with him, the whole human race appears to my no doubt partial imagination, as drawn with inferior colours, & endowed with inferior intellectual powers — For more than twenty years, he was the idol of my heart, the centre of my earthly happiness, & altho deprived of his dear society above nine years absence it never for one moment weaned my affection. I must not however pursue this theme, but endeavour if possible to give you some little account of that malady which terminated a life so valuable, not only to myself but to society in general — A complaint in the bladder, the foundation of which was no doubt laid during his

124

confinement in the Isle of France, but which he had in a great measure got the better of, returning at intervals in the beginning of last winter, brought on by unremitting attention to his work, an attention so close, that he neither allowed himself recreation, nor time for proper exercise, this sedentary mode of life totally undermined a constitution naturally good, and in Feb 2 he was seized with what was thought to be a severe fit at the time. In the course of a few days the pain abated, but left a constant sense of uneasiness in the region of the bladder, medical aid was called in but Alas! to no good purpose, the disease gradually gained ground, & at length worn out by the effects of this most distressing malady, he sunk under it & fell a martyr to the service of his country, as much as tho he had expired in battle — He just lived to know, the work over which his life had been spent was laid before the World, for he left this earthly scene of things, a few days after its publication —

On being opened, his bladder was found in the most dreadful state of decay, the inner membrane was literally torn to shreds by an incalculable number of small crystals, which were found sticking in every part, the outer coat was become so thickened by inflammation & constant irritation that it was incapable of containing more than half a wine glass of fluid—

In the last few weeks of his illness, had you seen your friend my Dear Sir, you would not have recognised him; so dreadfully was he altered, he looked full 70 years of age, &

was worn to a skeleton — Thus my dear Sir, I have given
you some faint account of the last days of my departed, best
loved friend, the recital has cost me many tears.

. . . I remain your greatly obliged,
Ann Flinders

The crystals were probably not the direct cause of Matthew's death; it was more likely to have been a massive urinary tract infection caused by the crystals piercing the soft internal tissues. For want of something as simple as water, Matthew Flinders' last weeks, and indeed his life, ended painfully and prematurely.

He left an estate valued at £3,498.16.1d. Unrealistically, his will had made provision for bequests well in excess of this amount — among them £326.10.1d for bills due, £73.16.0d for funeral costs, £14.6.0d for mourning rings and £101.3.6d for a monument at Donington — leaving Ann struggling to find £50 to complete the publication of his volumes. In the first print-run of *A Voyage to Terra Australis*, 121 of the 150 imperial size copies were sold, as were 1,000 small copies. The income generated was £2,666.13s.0d; the total expenses, £2,717.16s.3d. The Admiralty did not bother, or did not think it worthwhile, to distribute the charts to their captains. Yet in nearly two hundred years, subsequent navigators have not substantially altered Flinders' charts, and even today they are widely acclaimed, as are '*his accounts also of wind, weather, climate, currents, and tides* [which] *are excellent.*'

On Matthew's death, application was made to the Admiralty to grant a special pension to his widow. (The widow of Captain James Cook had been granted a pension of £200 per year.) Sir

Joseph Banks extended his championing of Matthew Flinders to the young widow, but although he had been a formidable and influential patron in his day, and had been head of the Royal Society for many years, his time of influence had now waned. It was to no avail.

Much later the application was brought to the attention of William IV, who agreed that Mrs Flinders should receive the same treatment as Mrs Cook. The King referred the application to an unsympathetic Lord Melbourne, with whom it rested, unacted upon to this day.

Ann was paid a post captain's widow pension until her own death in 1852. No reward, nor any recognition of the achievements of Matthew Flinders, was made by the British Government during her lifetime.

The Australian colony was more generous, and on their hearing of her plight, Ann was finally awarded a pension of £100 per year from the Government of New South Wales and a similar £100 from the Government of Victoria. The news of this gesture reached England in 1853, sadly the year after she died. Nevertheless, the pension deed was such that her daughter was able to use it to educate Matthew Flinders' young namesake, born that year. (It was money well spent, for Ann and Matthew's grandson, [Sir] William Matthew Flinders Petrie, was to achieve great renown in his own right as Britain's most distinguished Egyptologist, an explorer of a different world.)

Some time after Matthew's passing, Ann's mother came to live with her, Ann's stepfather, the Reverend Tyler, having died in 1808. Forever plagued by financial uncertainty, Ann was to move house fifteen times during the thirty-eight years she lived after Matthew's death, always carrying with her from house to house, and up and down narrow stairways, his old and familiar sea chest in which she stored her most valued possessions — his private papers and loving letters.

Perhaps as a result of her father's dramatic death at sea and Matthew's early demise, Ann often focused inordinately on her own health and that of her family. Hers was not a robust constitution, but she was not unhappy in her old age, being well attended in her later years by both her daughter Anne and her half-sister Isabella Tyler.

She found solace in the gentle arts, in singing and in writing verse, and in the peaceful pursuit of watercolourings of flowers, which she loved to collect and paint from nature. She copied, too, the botanic specimens of Terra Australis which Sir Joseph Banks had gathered on his voyage to the southern continent with Captain Cook. Over time she became an exquisite watercolourist with her more remarkable flower paintings dating from the period after Matthew's death. They are all the more remarkable considering the limited sight she had in one eye. Lack of funds to purchase paper for her watercolourings meant that whenever possible she used the backs of Matthew's drafts of his journal, and today her paintings present double-sided value, making interesting reading as well as viewing.

Ann wrote regularly to Pitot, and he to her, in the ensuing years. She assisted him by forwarding a subscription to the *Times* newspaper, political books and papers and sheet music. She also pursued the outcome of Pitot's court proceedings against the

One of Ann's finely wrought watercolourings

Admiralty on a long-standing matter. In the December following
Matthew's death she wrote to him:

My dear Sir,

*I addressed a letter to you in September last with an
account of the dreadful calamity which has befallen me, in
the loss of my ever to be lamented husband — a loss of
incalculable magnitude to me whose greatest earthly
happiness centred in him — My prospect in life is changed
indeed, now every thing around me wears a sombre aspect,
& but for the sake of my little darling Girl, I could lie
me in the silent tomb where rests the sad remains of Him
my heart once idolised. Time & Heaven, I trust will give
me resignations. At present I seem to feel daily more &
more the loss I have been called to endure. I must not
however indulge in this theme, but as I am pressed for
time, inform you on matters of business . . . Mr Nicol has
applied to a noted letter printer who has been accustomed
to fitting up printing presses for sending abroad, I therefore
hope it will not be long now before this business is settled
— the Writings & accounts relative to the proceedings in
the court of Admiralty, I have given into the hands of
Messrs Morris & Renny . . . — I shall forward some
newspapers to you, as also letters to Messres Chazal,
Dusbassayns & Labouve — I now send to you . . . three
months newspapers, with some Harp strings & music for
that . . . What I have sent, I procured at once at the finest
music shops in London, & I am assured that they are the*

most approved pieces of the day. I shall send to you all the flute music I can find, which belonged to Capt Flinders, some of which he purchased since he returned to England. The letters & bills exchange for Messrs Henskill & Co, I give into their hands, so soon as I see them.

I have consulted the Trustees respecting the little property Capt F left in the Isles of France & Bourbon. They are of the opinion that the cattle under Mr L's care had best be disposed of, & the amount remitted to England by the first safe opportunity. You perhaps would have no objections, to receiving the value of them, & allowing me to deduct it from the money of yours in my hands. This would save the trouble of remitting it. The money in Bourbon we are of opinion had best remain where it is, some time longer . . .

There is one circumstance I feel it necessary to mention to you, as I shall do also to Messrs D & L. Mr F, the brother of Capt F is I am sorry to observe, a character widely differing from your late friend, & one whom I find inclined to be very troublesome. He is I believe greatly mortified, at not being left Executor, but his brother had very sufficient reasons for cutting him off from all concern in his affairs. It is very possible he may write to you, but it is not necessary that you should render any account of the little property left in your Islands by Capt F to any person save myself . . . because I think it not improbably but Mr F may write to you in the names of the other Trustees.

Letters to Ann

My little darling Girl grows much & is become very entertaining. She is, if you can credit the word of a Mother, very articulate, intelligent. She often reminds me of her dear father. The upper part of her face being very like his, & I flatter myself she will inherit his noble integrity of character, & the amiability of his disposition. She is perfectly familiar with your name & very often talks of writing to Mr Thomy Pitot.

I remain Sir,
Ann Flinders

London St
Dec 15th 1814   *Sent by Messrs Marshall & Co.*

Ann and Matthew's daughter, Anne, was much petted and cherished in childhood. The outpourings of her mother's love and grief flowed into the child. The petted daughter grew into an affectionate but self-willed and strong-tempered woman. She shared her mother's love of music and poetry, and was to publish several small volumes of tales and poems. As a child she was delicate and nervous, and her health ill-managed by the family doctor. She suffered from nosebleeds and on as many as three occasions almost bled to death from leeches, for she was haemophilic. She contracted scarlet fever at fourteen and was prone to '*a congestion of the brain from overwork and studies*'. She took after her father with her habit of turning pale in the open air. She had another curious habit — an alarming one for those not familiar with it — of falling asleep so suddenly and soundly when very tired or in pain that it appeared she had fainted.

She had strange and vivid dreams, dreams which were said to be eerily prophetic in their nature, though what they foretold is no longer known.

Her mother, Ann, lived until her eightieth year. The headaches which had tormented her from middle age became more frequent and more violent as she grew older. Family records tell that she suffered regularly from pleurisy and that she died from old age and pneumonia, aged 79¼ years (according to family records) on 10th November 1852. Isabella wrote at the time of Ann's death:

Could she have chosen the circumstances of her decease she would not have wished it to have been different than it was, in her own home, her bed surrounded by those who she most loved, knowing us all, she gently laid her head on her pillow and fell into a gentle sleep from which she did not wake. Although through life she had endured many trials, heavy pecuniary losses and various disappointments she had the satisfaction of seeing her beloved and only child married to a man of piety and integrity, whose character she esteemed and approved.

Her grandson, William Matthew Flinders Petrie, noted in the family records, *'her early life was happy, her married life very sad . . . she suffered much.'*

Ann Flinders Chappelle was buried at St Thomas Rectory, Mary Road, Old Charlton, London. The date of her death, inscribed in a tablet in the south wall of the churchyard, shows her passing nine months earlier than the family records indicate.

Matthew Flinders Esquire

POST CAPTAIN, ROYAL NAVY

The Australian Discoverer

Died July 19, 1814, aged 40

And was Buried at St James Chapel,

Hampstead Road

the tomb having been destroyed

or removed before the year 1854.

This tablet erected to his memory

Also to that of

Ann,

his widow

Daughter of Captain John Chappelle,

Who died February 10, 1852;

and was buried in this churchyard.'

The two sisters, so close in life, were buried in the same grave —
Isabella following Ann some fifteen years later.

What I now and must ever feel

Detail from a painting showing Ann in her later years

Memoir by Ann Flinders

Among those exalted characters whom Providence in its bounty has raised up at various periods in the history of Man, — who by the exersions of superior genius, or the successful applications of eminent talent, have at once enlightened & advanced the age in which they lived — the experienced navigators, the explorer of new regions, who forsaking the safe comforts of domestic happiness, voluntarily devotes the prime of his life to the hazardous enterprises of discovery — thus opening to the scientific & mercantile world new fields of research, & the attainment of riches, surely deserves no inconsiderable place in the estimation of the wise & good -

In this number of public benefactors, may justly be ranked Captain Matt^w Flinders, the subject of the following Memoirs, which while they briefly exhibit his progress from the earliest period of life, to its disastrous termination, is largely the result of his labours before the world, must from the adventurous spirit, & unconquerable perseverance they display, render his Memory interesting to every feeling mind & lover of science: with such a Man we must naturally sympathise in every vicissitude, & those Navigators whose unremitting exersions have contributed to the acquiring of useful knowledge & of commerce, are particularly entitled to our esteem -

Matt" Flinders, eldest Son of Matt" & Susanne Flinders, was born on the 16ᵗʰ of March 1774 at Donington in L — which is about 20 miles from Grantham, justly celebrated as the birthplace of the great Sir Isaac Newton — His Father, a Man of education, & excellent moral habits, was esteemed for his abilities as Surgeon of Donington, & his grand-father & great-grandfather had successfully practiced physic in that Neighbourhood — Being designed to follow the profession of his father, after preparing some years at an excellent free school in Donington, he was at the age of twelve years sent to a Grammar School at Warbling, then kept by the Revd Mr Shingler — here he acquired a competent knowledge of the greek & latin classics, & after continuing there about 3 years, was taken home by his father in order to initiation in the mysteries of physic — During the time he was at home, which was rather more than 12 months, not much relishing the profession for which he was designed, (a trial of which he had made both at home & at Lincoln, whither his father had sent him for the purpose) he, partly by stealth, read Robinson Crusoe, that celebrated book of which Rousseau speaks so highly in his Emile, & to which perhaps more than any other, Great Britain is indebted for many of her numbers of enterprising & skilful Naval Officers, as well as numbers of her best & most experienced seamen, the effects produced on the young Man of our Adventurer will be, in part conceived by the following circumstances -

He immediately wrote to his cousin John Flinders, then in the West Indies, who had served his time under Admiral Gardner & Appleck, when he stated in answer, 'the little chance there was of *success in the Naval Service, without powerful interest; & that he himself had served nearly 11 years, & then had but small hopes of obtaining a Lieut^{nt} commission,'* but the ardour of our young seaman was not to be damped; & he attended more to the advice contained in the latter part of the letter, viz 'to study Euclid, & Robertson's* Elements *& to make himself well acquainted with Moore's* Navigation' *than to the long services & disappointments of his Cousin — He seriously set himself to work, made himself acquainted with Euclid, studied Robertson's* Elements; *& before a year had elapsed, unassisted by any one, he had so far mastered Hamilton Moore that his knowledge in Trigonometry, & the practical part of Navigation, astonished & surprised the schoolmaster of his native Town — At this period, May 1790, being then 16 years of age, & having received some encouragement from a female Cousin to follow up his intentions & who was at that time Governess to the two daughters of Captain, afterwards Admiral Sir Thomas Pasley, on presenting himself as a volunteer on board the* Scipio, *lying at Chatham, he was firstly received by that Officer; put on the quarter-deck & afterwards accompanied him on being appointed to H.M.S.* Bellerophon *— but the causes for which the Spanish, or rather the Russian armament had been made, having ceased; & an expedition being fitted out under Captain, now Admiral Bligh, for the purpose of fetching the Breadfruit & other plants from the Friendly Islands to the British West Indies, & as our adventurer could never bear the thought of inactivity, in 1791 with the permission of his patron Captain Pasley he embarked on board the* Providence, *from which time may be dated that passion for discovery, which never left him during life — In this voyage it is* *believed, he proved to Captain Bligh a useful acquisition, by being ever ready to assist him in his charts & astronomical observations; so much so that in the latter part of the voyage, altho' so young a Man, the observation & the care of the Time Keepers were principally entrusted to him — On returning home in the latter part of 1793, he again joined Commodore Pasley in the* Bellerophon, *& in the action of the memorable 1st of June was Aide de Camp to that brave distinguished officer. No little circumstances frequently give more real insight into character than the enhanced account of more publick actions, it is hoped the following brief anecdote will not be disappointing to our readers. On Lord Howe breaking the French Line on that decisive day, the 2nd or 3rd ship from the* Queen Charlotte *was the* Bellerophon; *her guns mounted beam on 3 of the Enemys Ships, & some of those on the quarter deck, having been left loaded & primed by their men to attend on their mainsails Mr Flinders, having at that time no orders but to fire away as fast as possible, seized the lighted match, & at the instant his ship was passing under the stern of a large French three-decker, fired off in succession as many of the deserted guns as would bear, right into her: Commodore Pasley having observed his actions, shook the young hero violently by the collar & sternly said 'How dare you do this, youngster without my orders' Mr F immediately replied he 'did not know, but he thought it was a fine chance to have a good shot at 'em' — After returning to Port from this battle, being still fonder of discovery than the regular line of service, in July or August 1794 our Navigator joined HMS* Reliance, *commanded by Captain Henry Waterhouse, formerly 5th Lieutenant of the* Bellerophon; *& in* Reliance *Capt now Admiral Hunter was to embark, as Governor of the young* colony at P Jackson, on the coast of New South Wales. In this voyage it appeared to our Adventurer that opportunities of following his favourite pursuit would frequently occur; & in this he was not disappointed, for where they did not happen he made, pointed them out to the Governor & faithfully executed his intentions.

It was not however until the 15 of Feb 1795 that the Reliance quitted Plymouth, in company with Earl Howe, the grand fleet, & perhaps the greatest number of merchant ships for different destinations that ever quitted the english shores — Previous to sailing, as his absence was likely to be for a number of years he paid a visit to his friends in Lincolnshire; when finding his brother Samuel had a mind to follow in his career, he prevailed on his father to let him join him in the Reliance as a Volunteer -

In Sept 1795 He arrived at Port Jackson, & suffered only a month to lapse before he & his friend Mr G Bass Surgeon of the Reliance, being unable to procure any better equipment, in a little boat of eight feet long, called Tom Thumb, began operations; Entered Botany Bay, & explored Georges River 20 miles further up than it had been carried by Governor Hunter's survey. But to give an account of the different excursion, hazardous undertakings in boats & small vessels as well as the miraculous escapes of our daring adventurer during nearly 5 years' stay of the Reliance in the Service of the Colony would exceed the limits of this hasty sketch of his life, as well as anticipate the pleasure the reader will have in pursuing the voyage itself: he is therefore referred to the introduction of the Voyage to Terra Australis, now before the publick, where from pages 97 to 204 of the Introduction, he will be satisfied that, amid difficulties insurmountable to other men, no opportunity was lost, or stone left *unturned to further the promotion of geographical knowledge in this new & interesting Country. Indeed so strong was his Inclination for this dangerous service that amongst his friends, he has been frequently heard to declare his belief 'That if the plan of a Discovery Expedition were to be read over his grave, he would rise up awakened from the dead' — For the successful pursuit of his favourite employment, his voyage in the* Investigator *will offer the best proof, &, forever remain an example of his undaunted spirit & irresistible perseverance: In him, prudence, ability, & the most unswerved industry were united in an uncommon manner: no difficulty could stop his career, no danger dismay him: hunger, thirst, labour, rest, sickness, shipwreck, imprisonment, Death itself, were equally to him matters of indifference if they interfered with his darling Discovery. After his shipwreck, on returning 730 miles in an open boat to the Colony of Port Jackson, the governor & officers greeted him with the name of Indefatigable — a title which it may be expected he will ever merit at his country's hands. But as a man's life & merits are but learnt from his works, the Publick, for an account of these, is referred to the very interesting voyage which he had just completed & given to the world, previous to his lamented dissolution. Little now remains to the Author of these memoirs but to refer the reader to a short statement of its objects, published in the monthly magazine for Oct 1807 — to state his advancement to rank in his profession; & to give a brief account of the circumstances attending his untimely end. He passed his examination at the Cape of Good Hope in 1797, & was appointed in a vacancy acting Lieut of HMS Reliance, by Governor Hunter, on her second arrival at Port Jackson: this appointment, he principally attributed to the kind offices of his friend, Captain Wm*

Hunt who well I knew his merit, & it was afterwards confirmed by the Admiralty; which circumstance he always thought arose, from some favourable representation of his first Patron, Admiral Sir Thomas Pasley.

On the return of HMS Reliance to England, in the latter part of 1800, such were the useful services he had rendered to Navigation, & geography in New Holland, & such the Charts & information he laid before that great Patron of useful knowledge the Right Hon*ble* Sir Joseph Banks, one of His Majesty's Privy Council, & this gentleman, after writing to the Admiralty on the subject of further Discoveries, interested himself so much that another voyage was set on fast; & in the early part of 1801 Lieut Flinders was appointed to the command of the Xenophon, then lying at Sheerness under orders to prepare for this service. Her name was changed to the Investigator by directions from the Admiralty, & previously to sailing Lieut*nt* F rec*d* the rank of Master & Commander.

In April he married Ann, daughter in law of the Rev*d* & Mrs Tyler of Partney in Lincolnshire; her own father, whose name was Chappelle, died at sea when commanding a vessel out of Hull in the Baltic trade. By her husband left issue an orphan daughter, two years old & had ill provided for by the scanty property she had attained by his merits & long services in his hazardous profession -

In July 1801 he sailed from England; successfully completed his voyage, for which see the work itself, where in about 18 months, he circumnavigated & accurately examined the coasts of Terra Australis, an island little inferior to all Europe; & on the 17th of August 1803 was shipwrecked on an unknown Coral Reef, 200 miles from the main land & 730 from the Colony of Port Jackson

— *This he however surmounted; made the necessary arrangements
with his officers on the Bank, in case of his loss; conducted an open
boat to the settlement — procured from Governor King & safely
conducted a vessel to the fatal reef sufficient to convey his officers &
people to China; & still persevering in his intention of getting himself
& his valuable Discoveries to England with all possible expedition
crossed the great South Sea in a little schooner of 27 tons burthen,
called the* Cumberland; *when on the very day 4 months on which it
was unfortunately wrecked (ie on the 17th of Dec^r) he entered Port
Louis in the Isle of France: Here in the truth of his passport he was
unjustly retained, & cruelly lingered out an imprisonment of six
years & a half — At length, on his return to his motherland, in
October 1810, he was promoted to the rank of Post Captain, & Mr
Yorke, the then 1st Lord of the Admiralty was good enough to date
his commission as far back as the time he came into office 7th May
1810. From the letters & representations which passed on the subject
it would appear that this was all that could be done; although Mr
Yorke acknowledged that had Captn F arrived in England safely
with his charts & discoveries in 1804, he would at that time have
merits & been entitled to the rank he then held — so that in addition
to the misfortune of shipwreck — of being nine years cast off from
society & the bosom of his family, six of which by cruel & unjust
imprisonment while employed in his country's service — he was by this
last stroke made to feel that this, instead of obtaining for him any
extraordinary reward for his services, had in reality deprived him of
six years of that rank in the Navy to which he was so justly entitled
— Neither were any of his Lieut^{ns} who had been shipwrecked, but not
imprisoned, promoted for their services⁺ — In the beginning of 1811*

Captain F altho not continued in full pay, was directed by the Admiralty to write an account of his voyage & discoveries: this object after immense labours, by depriving himself of the necessary exercise conducive to health, curtailing his natural rest, & sitting closely to it, he completed & in less than two months afterwards died, on the 19th of July last at the age of 40 years — Thus in the prime of life, fell an officer unexampled in his devotions to the service of his country — from the age of 16 to 40, a period of 24 years, he served it faithfully & unremittingly — never for twenty years, or until his arrival in England from imprisonment having been unemployed, or on half pay, not even a single day & never allowing himself in his visits to his family & friends more than three weeks absence from his duty — if the six years & a half passed in imprisonment & four years constantly occupied in laying his labours before the World, by orders from the Admiralty, be not looked upon in that light -

(⁺Note: Mr Fowler his 1st having obtained his present rank through other channels & other services; whilst Capⁿ F's brother, his 2nd who independent of his duty of lieutenant, also filled the department of Astronomer, was left unnoticed, nor could any representations of his get him the step his brother was convinced he deserved. It appears that this officer, the 2nd Lieutenant, whilst commanding the Bloodhound, *had been tried by a Court Martial for disobedience of orders, & thro the circumstances of a pilot who had neglected his duty, was found guilty; degraded of 3 years rank; & dismissed from the command of his vessel; — so that all his former services went for nothing — nor could any representation of his brother or Commodore Owen, under whom he was then serving under do away the obstacle to his*

advancement. *Should the Admiralty, now that Captain Flinders is no more, be desirous of paying respect to his memory (As they cannot probably step out of the regular course in allowing his widow an extraordinary pension, nor as his child is a female at some future period bring it forward in the Navy) it may occur to the 1ˢᵗ Lord, that there is still one being in existence whom it would have highly gratified Captⁿ F to see promoted for his services in the* Investigator; *and that whatever his fault might have been in regard to the court martial, as he has been severely & long punished for them, his former services ought perhaps in Justice to humanity to be rewarded by the attainment of that rank he would otherwise have been entitled to: more particularly as no instance can be produced wherein Lieutˢ in other voyages of discovery have not been promoted & when it is notorious that Lieutⁿ & even midshipmen in the French voyages the rival of the* Investigator's *are now Captⁿ de vessels, Captⁿ de Frigate & one of them made an Admˡ by our rivals in science & arms.)*

His complaint on being opened was found to be disease of the kidneys, but more particularly of the bladder, which was discovered more to resemble a mass of fibrous strings & honeycombed sponge than anything like the human organ, & was believed by the faculty to have been occasioned by want of exercise, long sitting & sedentary habits — the foundation was probably laid in the Reliance, *from the length of time he employed in perfecting his* <u>first</u> *charts of New Holland or Terra Australis* — From close imprisonment in the Isle of France it became confirmed & at times was excruciatingly painful, & altho' he afterwards had intervals of ease, yet the last four years of sedentary life in sitting to prepare his labours for the public eye was

145

too much for his, or perhaps any constitution to resist, & he died if ever Man did, a martyr to his zeal for his country's service — That Country it is hoped will properly appreciate, & long retain the memory of his services & the learned & scientific of other Nations will deplore the loss of a Man whose life has been spent in useful research, & whose last days were devoted to laying the result of his labours before the world — Geography & Navigation will severely feel the loss: for who of his countrymen, after his shipwreck, imprisonment, & death, will now venture on such pursuits? — Among the young of his profession who would encounter the arduous task, few perhaps none profess the ability successfully to pursue in his career, & among the old, who have the ability, perhaps not one may be found willing, by altering his mode of life, to exchange ease & security, for the dangerous presentations of Voyages of discovery — It may however afford some consolation to his family & friends to believe that the name of <u>Flinders</u> will henceforth stand equal in the annals of discovery, with a Dampier, a Wallis or a Byron; equal perhaps with the later & more celebrated names of a Bougainville, a Bligh, a Penzanse, or even with that of the immortal Cook — This private character was as admirable as his public one, his integrity, uprightness of intention, disdain of deception & liberality of sentiment, wise not to be surpassed, & he possessed all the social virtues & affections in an eminent degree -

+ It is however but justice to the memory of Admiral Appleck to state, that after being long his follower, he was made a Lieut[nt] — & appointed to the Cygnet ship of war, on board of which, he died from after of the Yellow Fever in the West Indies.

CHRONOLOGY

Matthew Flinders

Date of birth	..	16 March 1774
Birthplace	..	Donington, Lincolnshire
Occupation	..	Royal Navy
Residences	..	At sea; 6 years prisoner in Mauritius, last 4 years in London
Age at marriage	..	26 or 27
Mode of life so far as affecting growth or health	..	Usual hardships of sea life. Severe anxiety, and hot climate during imprisonment.
Adult height	..	5ft 7?
Colour of hair when adult	..	Dark
Colour of eyes	..	Dark brown
General appearance	..	Slight and active, pale complexion
Bodily strength and energy	..	Strength average. Extreme energy and activity.
Keenness or imperfection of sight or other senses	..	Very keen senses and observation. Short-sighted late in life.
Mental powers and energy	..	Great talent for discovery and science, especially physical. Fond of Greek.
Character and temperament	..	Firm, just, punctual, clear-headed. Nicknamed 'Indefatigable'. Liberal and kind.
Artistic aptitudes	..	Drew maps with great accuracy. Played flute.
Minor ailments in youth	..	Measles and cough at 11 years of age
in middle age	..	A habit of turning deadly pale in the open air
Graver illnesses in middle age	..	Debility from hardships/climate. Cystic disease.
Cause and date of death	..	Died of above causes, 19 July 1814, aged 40.
General remarks	..	Was in Lord Hawes' action, went round the world on service, discovered South Australia and Bass's Strait, and surveyed nearly the whole coast (1801–4). Made prisoner by the French. Returned 1810, broken in health, and died in 1814.

Ann Chapelle

Date of birth	..	21 November 1772
Birthplace	..	Hull, Lincolnshire
Occupation	..	—
Residences	..	Hull, Partney, Barton, London, Southampton, Clifton, Reading, Woolwich
Age at marriage	..	28
Offspring	..	1 daughter
Mode of life so far as affecting growth or health	..	Easy and comfortable
Was early life laborious?	..	No
Adult height	..	5ft
Colour of hair when adult	..	Raven black, long and curly
Colour of eyes	..	Rich red brown
General appearance	..	Slight and graceful; pale complexion
Bodily strength and energy	..	Strength not great, energy considerable
Keenness or imperfection of sight or other senses	..	One eye blinded by lancing, in smallpox, the other good. Other senses good.
Mental powers and energy	..	Above average of her contemporaries — considered clever
Character and temperament	..	Sweet, perfect temper. Beloved by all who knew her. Witty. Generous. Nervous.
Artistic aptitudes	..	Poetry and literature. Singing. Wrote good verses. Painting flowers from nature.
Minor ailments		
in youth	..	Very delicate; brought up in the country
in middle age	..	Nervous ailments, from sorrows
Graver illnesses		
in youth	..	Smallpox at 12. Lost one eye, almost.
in middle age	..	Violent headaches. Pleurisy from 65, twice a year.
Cause and date of death	..	Decay of nature, and pneumonia. Died 10 Feb 1852, aged 79.
General remarks	..	Her early life was happy; her married life very sad. Her husband's absence for 9 years, at sea, and in prison in a hot climate, injured her health and nerves. Always patient and sweet, she suffered much. Her half sister and only child attended her to the last.

LIST OF SOURCES

Austin, K A, *The Voyage of the Investigator 1801–1803,* Rigby, 1964.

Australian Archives, Canberra, Australia.

Baker, Sidney J, *My Own Destroyer: A Biography of Capt. Matthew Flinders RN,* Currawong Publishing, Sydney, 1962.

Colwell, Max, *The Voyages of Matthew Flinders,* Paul Hamlyn, 1970.

Galton, Francis, *Family Faculties Manuscript,* 1883.*

Flinders Papers, Greenwich Maritime Museum.

Flinders Private Papers, Mitchell Library, Sydney.

Hibbert, Christopher, *The English: A Social History,* Grafton Books, 1987.

Ingleton, Geoffrey Chapman, *Matthew Flinders, Navigator & Chartmaker,* Genesis Publications in association with Hedley Australia, 1986.

Lincolnshire History and Archaeology Vol 23, 1988 'The Flinders family of Donington'.

Mack, James D, *Matthew Flinders 1774–1814,* Thomas Nelson, 1966.

Russell, R W, (ed.) *Matthew Flinders: The Ifs of History,* Flinders University, Adelaide, 1979.

Scott, Ernest, *Life of Matthew Flinders,* Sydney, Angus & Robertson, 1914.

Watkins, Susan, *Jane Austen's Town and Country Style,* Rizzoli, 1991.

* In 1883 the eugenicist Sir Francis Galton (a cousin of Charles Darwin) chose the Flinders family for a study to record in detail the physical appearance, health and emotional disposition of each member of the family so that comparisons could be made across a number of generations to assess the degree to which health and physical appearances were inherited down the generations.